Stress Relief for Women

Stress Relief
for Women

JANET WRIGHT

First published in 1997 by
Parragon
Unit 13–17
Avonbridge Trading Estate
Atlantic Road
Avonmouth
Bristol BS11 9QD

Copyright © Parragon 1996

Text previously published in *Essential Health for Women*,
hardback illustrated edition 1996,
paperback illustrated edition 1997

ISBN 0-75252-414-3

Designed by Sandie Boccacci

Janet Wright started work as a newspaper reporter in London, covering crime, conflict and disaster. Since she was more interested in routes to well-being, she started writing features specializing in health. She became freelance after working for *Health & Fitness* and *Prima*, Britain's top-selling women's monthly magazine.

Earlier, she took a lorry-ride to Africa that turned into a six-year career break while she travelled around the world, fascinated by the ways other people live and care for their health. She financed her explorations with casual work (more farms, offices and kitchens than she cares to remember) as well as teaching English in China and working for an Aboriginal group in central Australia.

On the way, she found that most people are better at relaxing than we are in the western world – even in harsh conditions. She hopes to help change this!

Janet Wright has written extensively on health, self-help and well-being. She relaxes using many of the methods in this book, as well as riding her motor-bike.

Contents

How to Use this Book

Almost all the techniques in this book can be tried at home, so it's full of easy exercises and do-it-yourself tips. Some of them will be all you need. Others, if you like them, you can go on to learn more fully in a class or buy a book on the subject.

Where no exercises are given, it's because the technique really needs to be taught personally by a trained expert. In the 'Where Do I Go From Here?' pages at the end there's a list of organizations and books for further information.

What Causes Stress?

The modern Western way of life could have been designed to cause early heart attacks. But not many of us have the chance to go and live on a tropical island – and we'd probably miss a lot if we did. The more practical answer is to make the most of living here and cut down on the stress.

FEELING STRESSED doesn't mean that you're neurotic. It's a perfectly natural response to events that threaten our safety. At the first sign of danger, our whole metabolism switches onto a war footing. We stop digesting food or making internal repairs. Our bodies are flooded with adrenaline and other emergency hormones to rush oxygen around the body and release quick-energy fuel into the bloodstream. For a few minutes we're the strongest and fastest we can possibly be – just long enough to spear that wolf or run away from that landslide.

That's the trouble: the stress response was designed for a time when danger was deadly but brief. It's just as proficient today, for the record-breaking leap to stop a toddler pulling a hot saucepan down on her head, but more often that heart-thudding rush happens when we're stuck in a traffic jam or faced with a bill that we can't pay. Unused, the stress hormones linger in our bodies, wreaking havoc on our health.

These days we tend to have long-term problems. We want some control over our lives, but things are changing all around us and sometimes we're swept along with the tide. Jobs are insecure, marriage is no longer a life-long commitment, our food and environment are increasingly polluted, we work longer hours than ever before, it's hard to make ends meet and the world seems full of dangers to our children. Relationships and family problems add to our list of worries. We feel responsible for everyone's well-being but powerless to make everything all right, every time. All this is a recipe for stress.

Learning to relax

Do we really need to learn how to relax? Look at a cat asleep by the fire – no one taught it how to flop into instant sleep or wake up with a long and sensuous stretch, ready for anything. But when did you last feel so relaxed? The trouble is that human beings have a far more complicated life than cats.

Somewhere between inventing the wheel and weaving the Internet we've forgotten most of what cats know about staying healthy. Babies still know – but as we go out into the speedy, competitive adult world, it all slips away. Until we start feeling exhausted, troubled by niggling pains or unaccountably near to tears, we don't even realize we've lost something we need.

The techniques in this book are just as good for either sex. But women often tend to have more responsibilities and less time or money to spend on their own needs. Though most of us now do a paid job as well as running a home, the figures show we still do almost all the housework and childcare. An ever-increasing number are doing the whole lot by themselves. Women are brought up to care about everyone else and, when time's at a premium, looking after themselves is the easiest task to drop.

So some of the tips in this book are ten-second lifesavers – for moments of crisis or when you simply can't take the break you need.

Relaxation is a powerful medicine. It speeds recovery from all kinds of illnesses and, better still, can help prevent them in the first place. It magics away the pain caused by muscles that we didn't even realize were tensed up like fists. It relieves stress in its many and varied physical manifestations, from indigestion to heart disorders. It keeps us young, not only smoothing out the lines etched into our faces but giving us years of healthier, more active life. It brings back the sort of energy that we used to take for granted – how often have you watched children playing and thought 'Was I ever as lively as that?' In short, it makes life a lot more enjoyable.

Most of us think we could relax perfectly well if we had more time. Yet when there is time, what do we do? Collapse in front of the television, even when there's nothing we want to watch, because we're too tired to do anything that we'd enjoy more, or there's no one to look after the children. Then, disturbed by the news and frazzled by canned laughter, we sleep badly and wake up more tired than ever.

A week on a health farm might do us all good. But that's not the only route to relaxation, by a long way. Take your pick from techniques that are sociable or solitary, a two-minute pick-me-up or a two-hour ritual, quick to learn or part of a long-term investment in your future, recommended by doctors or taught by spiritual leaders, invented for modern needs or as old as time. This book looks at dozens of options, especially ones that are cheap and simple. Relaxation isn't yet another task to fit into a crowded day. It's about finding ways that you enjoy and that will work for you.

The Unrelaxers

We've all got favourite ways of relaxing, but some are more effective than others and some aren't really relaxing at all. Let's be honest – flopping in front of the television can be just the job after a day spent running after children and speeding round the shops. But edge-of-the-seat games shows and horror films can leave your heart pounding like a woodpecker. And if you've spent an equally tiring day sitting at a desk, more sitting is just what you don't need.

FOR MANY WOMEN, a coffee or cigarette break is the only chance that they get to stop working. But caffeine and nicotine are stimulants, not relaxers. The short break is actually to 'unrelax', to take chemicals on board that will help you stay alert a bit longer. However, they do just the same when you've finished work, and are trying to wind down. They are addictive, so having one is a relief because it stops the craving.

But while sitting down to a familiar ritual can be relaxing in itself – the caffeine and nicotine whizzing round your bloodstream keep everything hyped up (and even tea contains some caffeine) – herbal teas, or the beverages sold in health food shops, are a better bet for relaxing.

Alcohol is famous for helping people relax – often more than they intended to. But though it can ease stress, unknot tense muscles and bring on sleep, the benefits are only temporary – you'll breathe shallowly and wake up early. Beware, too, if you start finding that you can't relax without it.

Not all drugs are equal, of course. A drink or a couple of coffees a day shouldn't do any harm unless you're pregnant or have been warned off them by your doctor. Some researchers even recommend a glass of wine a day to keep the heart healthy. Tobacco, on the other hand, offers no benefits of any kind. It's harmful even in small amounts and – never mind dying young – causes more boring, painful, totally avoidable ill-health than anything else in the Western world. Relaxing with a cigarette is like trying to sleep on a bed of nails – it causes stressful reactions such as speeding up your heart, so the body can't relax deeply. It's expensive too, saving the cost of a packet of cigarettes a day will pay for a genuinely relaxing weekly treat. If you're worried about putting on weight, healthy eating and exercise will keep it off.

Overeating is another false friend when you're under stress. Don't feel guilty, just find more helpful ways of being kind to yourself when you need it.

Tranquillizers may seem the only answer when you're desperate, but these addictive drugs only help for a short time, if at all. After that, they cause more damage than they could ever have cured. If you're at the end of your tether, ring the Samaritans – listed in your local phone book – or ask your doctor to refer you for counselling or to put you in touch with one of the self-help groups set up by fellow-sufferers for all kinds of problems. These can also give sympathetic, practical advice if you're already hooked and need help coming off.

Standing up to stress

When something makes you feel stressed, there are three ways of reacting:
1. Change things outside, by taking action to solve the problem.
2. Change things inside, by accepting what's happening and coming to terms with it.
3. Do neither, and worry helplessly.

Needless to say, the first course of action is best, whether it's joining an environmental action group or refusing to clean up after everyone.

Some things can't be changed so, option 2, you simply have to live with them – any energy you put into resenting them is wasted.

Often, though, you can compromise with a mixture of 1 and 2. Take money, for example – that prime source of worry. You can try to earn more or spend less. Cut up credit cards and find new pleasures that don't cost anything, until the wheel of fortune turns back in your favour.

Contact anyone whom you owe money (especially if they own your home) and arrange to pay in manageable instalments.

Take whatever steps you can to protect yourself and your family, stay out of any more debt, look after your health, learn new skills that could earn extra cash.

Keep Worries in their Place

If you can't stop fretting over a problem:

- Make an appointment with it. Every afternoon, say, from 2.15 to 2.30, settle down and worry about it.

  Give it your full attention and get as upset as you need to.

  No, honestly – try it. If you don't feel comfortable sitting down to it, do it while you're ironing. But only for fifteen minutes – set a timer and stop when it buzzes. When you catch yourself worrying at other times, stop at once – but promise yourself you've only got to wait till 2.15.

- Wash it away. Worry to your heart's content while you're washing up or cleaning floors – but only then – and throw your worries out with the dirty water.

- Write it down. The whole dreadful story, and all the awful things that could happen. Then burn it or tear it into tiny pieces.

  The same when you're angry – write a steaming letter to the person who's upset you, then make sure you destroy it. Just don't send it!

And then stop worrying. Hard to do, yes, but not impossible. Meditation and breathing techniques are a big help here, creating a feeling of peace and calmness. And like any exercise, they get easier the more you practise.

Worry is worse than useless – its paralysing effects stop people doing anything constructive. It stops you enjoying what you've got. And it can cause a host of problems of its own, such as phobias and panic attacks.

Learning to relax clears the mind and frees up energy, making it easier to find solutions. The only answer is:

- Relax.
- Think what to do.
- Do it.
- Get on with your life.

Hormonal Upheaval

❊

No one can relax when they're suffering from premenstrual syndrome (PMS), which affects about three-quarters of us at one time or another. For most of us women it's a fairly mild nuisance – a bit of fluid retention making shoes and waistbands nip too tightly, a day or so when people seem unusually irritating or life looks bleak. Then our period starts and everything's back to normal. For some, though, it means major upheaval.

WILD MOODS, EXHAUSTION, unbearable depression, tension, confusion, insomnia and thoughts of violence or suicide – PMS has even been used as a defence in murder trials.

Since PMS is caused by a temporary imbalance in the female hormones (too much oestrogen or too little progesterone) and possibly an imbalance in brain chemicals too, the answer is to try to balance things out again.

If all else fails, some gynaecologists now give hormone treatment. But self-help methods tackle the problem rather than the symptoms – and without the side-effects of drugs.

- Even though you may feel bloated and depressed,

try to carry on as normal and be positive about life. This mood, as you well know, is temporary and will pass. It's not due to some earth-shattering event in your life, merely a passing biological imbalancer. So stop feeling self-pity, and get on with living.

Awareness of why you feel the way you do is half the battle won.

- Examine your feelings honestly, and see whether your depression isn't just an excuse not to stir yourself into action.

- Go for a walk. There is nothing like walking to lift your mood, and to get rid of that bloated feeling.

- Keep moving. Energetic exercise makes the body produce feel-good chemicals called endorphins. Women are often low on these the week before a period, which accounts for the low spirits.

- Try an aerobics class, go for a run with the dog or children, put on some lively music and dance all by yourself – anything to speed up your heart and get those endorphins moving.

- Eat little and often, especially if you find yourself wanting to nibble all the time. Instead of raiding the biscuit tin, have half a dozen small meals a day of wholesome carbohydrates like bread, pasta, fruit and vegetables. By keeping blood sugar levels steady, this helps prevent mood swings.

Eat to beat the blues

Changing your diet could solve PMS problems. Unfortunately, chocolate only cheers you up till you step on the scales – the solution is more likely to come in vegetable shape.

Modern convenience foods cause a lot of women's hormonal problems: they are packed with saturated fat, for instance, which makes the body produce too much oestrogen.

The Women's Nutritional Advisory Service (UK) finds that different kinds of PMS are caused, or made worse, by a shortage of nutrients. The service provides tailor-made anti-PMS diets, including food supplements if necessary, but also offers some general advice:

- To counteract all forms of PMS, stock up on vitamin B6 and magnesium. If your symptoms tend to be nervous tension, mood swings and anxiety, these may be all you need.

  For more vitamin B6, eat fish, liver, bacon, beans, yeast extract, tomato puree and bananas.

  For magnesium, add muesli, oatmeal, dried fruit and dried skimmed milk. There's plenty of both in wholemeal bread, soya flour, mung beans and nuts.

- To counteract weight gain, bloating and tender breasts, in addition to B6 and magnesium, add some vitamin E from oils (sunflower-seed, peanut, olive or cod-liver), nuts, salmon, tuna, blackberries, spinach and avocado.

- To counteract headaches, exhaustion, dizziness and craving for sweets, add chromium from rye bread, calf liver, eggs, brewer's yeast, peppers and potatoes.

- To counteract depression, confusion and insomnia,

you need vitamin C – weight for weight, there's even more in blackcurrants, parsley, canned guavas, strawberries, peppers and raw red cabbage than in oranges.

Peaceful Pregnancy

The image of a mother-to-be is a beautiful, tranquil creature drifting through soft-focus scenery, one hand on the neat little bump, the other stroking the head of a happy toddler. The reality, as most of us know or can guess, is rather different.

TODAY'S MOTHER-TO-BE is often either working until the last minute or caring for other children who aren't at all sensitive to her needs. The happy event may be overshadowed with financial worries or – especially if it's the first child – a secret fear that it might all be a terrible mistake.

Doubts and fears are perfectly natural. Having a child is, after all, a major change and a serious set of new responsibilities. Children restrict your freedom, make a mess, cost a fortune and never give you a day off. Bottling up these worries can cause a lot of unnecessary unhappiness, so talk it over with someone you trust.

Don't forget to welcome the new baby, though. It sounds bizarre, but many experts now believe the baby can sense your feelings about it. Unborn babies are certainly affected by their mother's moods, since these send hormones coursing through her blood-

Can You Hear Me In There?

- Sit comfortably with hands on your abdomen, maybe in a rocking chair, and talk to the baby growing inside you.
- Say something like, 'I'm looking forward to meeting you, and playing with you.'
- Tell it about the other members of the family, or what you've been doing that day. Just keep to positive subjects. You don't even have to talk out loud.
- What's happening is that you're encouraging your brain to produce calming, mood-lifting hormones.
- You'll feel good, and if the baby understands, all the better!
- Let its brothers and sisters listen to it through your tummy. This will help them to feel part of the process.

stream, which the baby shares. So when you're tense or angry the baby's going to be filled with the same stressful hormones.

Also, the baby hears and responds to noises just as we do. Researchers have even discovered their taste in music – they don't like heavy metal, but relax to serene sounds like Mozart.

- Give yourself time to relax every day, using any of the methods in this book. Easier said than done, but well worth the effort if you take the phone off the hook and tell everyone you're doing this for your health.
- Help the baby's father feel involved by giving you backrubs – or, even better, learning some massage

techniques. Lie on your side with a pillow supporting your upper knee as you get bigger. Avoid pressure on the abdomen (especially in the first few months) and only use essential oils if they're guaranteed safe for use in pregnancy. Also let him rub your legs gently upwards from the ankles.

- If your doctor wants to give you iron tablets, ask for a blood test to see if you really need them. If you do, look for liquid versions that claim not to cause constipation.
- As well as giving up smoking, try not to let anyone smoke near you. On top of everything else, it raises the levels of stress hormones in the blood.

Relax? With Kids like Mine?

*Bringing up children, with all its rewards, gives women
little chance to relax at the best of times. Looking after
hyperactive children makes it virtually impossible.*

SOMETIMES BAD BEHAVIOUR is caused by emotional
problems which call for counselling, preferably
on referral from a doctor. Homeopathy can also be
useful. Sometimes kids just need a grown-up to
spend time listening to them. And, of course, if they
see adults being angry they learn to do the same.
Local parents' groups can be helpful when you're
feeling isolated and under pressure.

With many children, though, one look at their
flushed faces and glazed eyes shows it's out of their
control. They look as if they've been drugged, and in
a sense they have. What with air pollution, passive
smoking and the use of chemicals in the food
industry, their small bodies can get a toxic overload.

Healthy eating helps children fight off the effects of
traffic fumes and other pollutants. If you live in an
old house with lead pipes in a soft-water area, let the
tap run fast for half a minute before using the water
first thing in the morning.

Some children are more sensitive than others to the
over-stimulating effects of nicotine, so try not to let

anyone smoke indoors, where fumes don't have a chance to disperse.

Many parents find the problem is caused by food additives. Once you know what foods contain a particular additive the connection may become obvious, when the child starts acting up straight after eating or drinking it. Occasionally a child is allergic to some normally wholesome food. If you suspect this, see an allergy consultant or ask your doctor to refer you to a dietician.

A surprising number of children simply don't eat enough – it's exhaustion that makes them so bad-tempered. Children who miss breakfast, in particular, get into more trouble at school and have lower exam results than those who start the day with a meal.

Snacking on junk food just makes matters worse, because it's full of things – like the caffeine in cola drinks and chocolate – that can make them moody and restless. Picky eaters are maddening, but perseverance pays off for everyone.

Several American prisons have reduced violence by giving inmates a healthier diet containing more magnesium, selenium and chromium and less sugar.

So try feeding your own tearaways on wholemeal bread, Marmite (brewer's yeast), leafy green vegetables, beans, onions, apricots, bananas and grapes.

Don't give vitamin or mineral supplements except in special formulations for children.

Get your Value in Vitamins and Minerals

Instead of junk food which tends to contain a lot of fat and sugar, which can make your child hyperactive, make sure you include the following nutritious foods in their diet.

Baked beans	complex carbohydrate, protein, fibre, sugar, iron, zinc, magnesium, thiamin, riboflavin, niacin, B6, sodium
Bananas	fruit sugar, fibre, protein, vitamin B6, folic acid, potassium
Cheese	protein, fat, calcium, riboflavin, vitamin B12, vitamin A, zinc, calcium
Chicken (grilled)	protein, riboflavin, niacin, thiamin, iron, zinc
Jacket potato	complex carbohydrate, protein, fibre, vitamin Bs, vitamin C
Oranges	fruit sugar, fibre, vitamin C, folic acid, potassium
Skimmed milk	protein, calcium, riboflavin, vitamin B12, zinc
Spinach	vitamins A, B6, C, E, riboflavin, calcium, folic acid, iron, magnesium, potassium
Wholemeal bread	complex carbohydrate, B vitamins, fibre, iron, zinc, magnesium, vitamin E
Wholemeal pasta	complex carbohydrate, protein, fibre, thiamin, niacin, B6, iron, vitamin E, zinc, magnesium

Soothing a Wild Child

- Add a few drops of calming aromatherapy oil like camomile or benzoin to a child's bath, mixed with a carrier oil for safety. This can aid a good night's sleep. A small child may accept being massaged with it. During the day, use it in an oil burner.
- Blue and green are calming colours for clothes and bedrooms. A hop pillow will help restless children sleep.
- Herbal teas – not heavily sugared herbal toddler drinks – can be soothing, if the child will drink them.
- Herbalist Penelope Ody recommends a weak 'tea' made with 10g of the herbs agrimony and self-heal in a mug of hot water, sweetened with honey.
- With herbs and oils, use quarter-strength for small children, half-strength when they're older. Don't let them put essential oils, even blended, in their mouths.

Moving with the Change

❧

Until recently, menopause was seen as a dreary time of health problems and endings. Now, luckily, women look at life more positively. There's no longer any need to define ourselves by our youth or ability to have children. Most of us will be working for at least another decade. Our activities, families and friends are there to help us through low times.

THE MENOPAUSE IS another of life's transitions, like your first day at school, puberty, setting up home and having children. Not all the changes are necessarily welcome. But this can be one of the most energetic times of a woman's life. Even old age needn't be frightening if you plan for it and look after your health.

Take exercise

Take some energetic exercise at least three times a week, to keep depression – and weight-gain – at bay. If it's also weight-bearing exercise (say aerobics or running) you'll be keeping your bones strong too. This reduces your risk of the brittle-bone disease osteoporosis, one of the major problems faced by older women.

Exercise

Try exercising for just ten minutes when you get up in the morning.

You will be amazed at the difference it makes, not just in keeping you supple, but in changing a perhaps depressed mood into a cheerful one.

You could start by doing the exercises shown on pp. 99–101.

Relax

When you feel stressed and irritable, find a quiet spot to do your favourite relaxation technique, take a walk or watch a cartoon video. Organize for your own needs instead of everyone else's.

Hormone Replacement Therapy (HRT)

Hormone replacement therapy helps some women, but find out about all the options. The Women's Nutritional Advisory Service offers natural alternatives.

Eat sensibly

Cut down on animal fats, coffee, fizzy drinks, sugar and alcohol but eat plenty of fresh vegetables and fruit. This will protect your bones as well as helping keep your moods on an even keel. Japanese women, who rarely suffer menopausal symptoms, eat masses of vegetables and soya products such as tofu (bean-curd).

Saying Goodbye

It's no use pretending losses aren't painful. Sometimes a letting-go ritual can help you say goodbye and move on.

Write a letter to the person or thing you've lost, whether it's your job, your marriage, your children who've left home, or anything else. Be clear what you're missing. If you're mourning your youth, for example, is it your fertility, your role as mother, your youthful looks? Or all of these? Do you suspect your sex life is over? Do you think you'll be despised and ignored? Do you fear weakness and ill-health?

Write it down without holding anything back. When you've got it all out, spend some time thinking it over and let yourself cry as much as you want. Then burn the letter and blow the ashes out of the window. Take a few deep breaths and say, 'I'm moving on to the rest of my life'. Then do something you enjoy, preferably with friends.

Be positive

The advice for PMS (page 12) is helpful for menopausal problems too.

Make time to go out with friends. If they've melted away over the years, find some more through evening classes or community groups. Talk problems over when you need to, but don't get into downbeat habits. Spend time with people who buck you up instead of bringing you down.

Promise yourself at least one thing a week that's nothing but fun. Look through the local paper for new things to do and book ahead.

Joy's wise woman's tonic

Good nutrition is particularly important for women, and especially so during the menopause when the body is readjusting to a new balance and afterwards to maintain health and strength.

Try this herbal recipe from Christopher Herron and Non Shaw's *Herbal Remedies*.

Calcium is found in parsley and cabbage, but for those needing an extra supplement try this tonic.

1 organic eggshell
juice of 1 lemon
15g/½ oz parsley, fresh or dried
15g/½ oz sage, fresh or dried
15g/½ oz fennel seed
2 teaspoons honey (optional)

Scrub the eggshell, remove the membrane from inside and crush the shell. Cover with lemon juice and leave to stand until the eggshell dissolves into a white sediment (2–3 days). Make 75 ml/2½ fl oz/⅓ cup of decoction (the extracted liquor resulting from the process of boiling down) from the herbs and add this to the mixture. Strain, add honey to taste if liked, and bottle.

To use: Shake well and take 2–3 teaspoons a day.

Coping with Pain

It's hard to relax when you're in pain, but that's when it does most good. Pain and tension fuel each other in a vicious cycle of distress. Relaxation is especially vital in conditions like backache when muscles go into spasm around the painful spot — that's meant to protect the area from further damage, but its main effect is to hurt even more.

ILLNESS IS A POWERFUL source of anxiety, and sometimes the treatments seem as disruptive as the disease. Though it's difficult to keep your mind on learning new techniques, this is a good time to take up relaxation. As well as speeding recovery, it could help prevent relapses.

- Try foot-to-head relaxation, meditation, visualizing yourself free of pain, plus any other techniques your doctor thinks suitable.
- Have you taken all practical steps to combat whatever's causing the pain?
- Go to your doctor if you have any unexplained pain — and get a second opinion if the first isn't helpful.

Mind over matter

Can you outwit pain or imagine it away? When nothing else is working or you don't want to fill yourself with painkillers, it's worth a try. It may take a while, but these methods have worked for many people.

- Lie or sit in any position you find comfortable and give yourself time.
- Start with some breathing exercises or meditation may help.
- Imagine a ray of light warming and healing the painful spot. Really feel the warmth and the comfort.
- See your pain as a wild animal, snarling and ferocious. Approach it safely – you're in control – then stroke it and soothe it till it calms down.
- Imagine the pain as something you can see – a rock, a blade, a blob of colour – and fix your attention on it. How big is it? What colour? What shape? Does it have a sound? A smell? Is it moving? The images will keep changing, but eventually you may wear it out. And by facing the pain you lose the fear that makes your muscles knot up so painfully.

Be kind to your back

Most women suffer backache at some time in their lives, what with periods, pregnancy, office work, high heels, carrying toddlers or just being on their feet all day.

Luckily there's a lot you can do to relieve it, especially by improving the way you stand and sit.

- A rucksack distributes weight more evenly than handbags or shoulder bags.
- For the same reason, use a baby sling or backpack-style carrier instead of toting Junior on your hip.
- If your bed's soft or more than ten years old you may be sagging while you sleep. Treat yourself to a firm new mattress.
- Make sure your work equipment – kitchen surfaces, office furniture – is the right height.
- Improve your posture, say with the Alexander Technique. Especially, tuck your tail under so the forward curve at your waist is slightly flattened. An exaggerated curve looks elegant but wrecks your spine.
- Bend your knees, not your back, to pick things up.
- Unless your doctor insists, staying active helps a bad back more than resting.
- Avoid any exercise that includes tipping your head backwards, straight-legged toe-touching or 'wind-milling', lifting both legs together or violent twists.
- Yoga, stretching and aerobic exercise can ease period-related backache.
- Ask your doctor if there's a local back-care clinic for more advice and special exercises.

Stress Relief First Aid

Many of the techniques in this book are quick and effective. Breathing exercises don't have to take more than a minute, and five minutes is enough to meditate or do a short foot-to-head muscle relaxation. While you're reading this book, why not put an 'x' in the margin beside your favourite quick relaxers so you can find them when you need them fast?

WHEN EVERYTHING'S getting on top of you, give yourself a break. That old advice about taking a deep breath still holds good – count to ten as you breathe out. If you're paralysed with anxiety, do a breathing exercise and clear your mind by concentrating on the feel of your breath. Start by blowing out hard to empty your lungs and let a deep breath in. If you feel faint, lie down with your feet higher than your head. If you feel like hitting someone, go for a walk instead.

Taking your mind off the problem can help – things are easier to cope with when you're not at the peak of stress. So read a light magazine feature or the stars (but only believe them if they're good). Make a cup of herbal tea and ring your best friend for some moral support. If you can't get the worry off your mind, put your brain to work recalling one of Shakespeare's sonnets, or counting backwards in threes from 100.

Meanwhile, here are some extra emergency tips.

Five seconds to spare

Just enough time for some encouraging affirmations – positive messages to the subconscious to boost your confidence.

- Silently tell yourself 'I'm doing well' and 'I can easily cope with all this'. Never mind if you don't believe it – say it as if you do.
- Repeat it a few times whenever you think of it. And if any mean inner voices start quibbling, imagine them coming from a radio and turn it off.

Ten seconds to spare

- Stand straight and breathe in through your nose as you stretch your arms above your head, palms together.
- As you start breathing out through your mouth, turn the palms out and slowly bring the arms down beside you, reaching out with the fingertips. As your arms come down, tell yourself 'I am perfectly calm'.
- If people are around, just pinch the web between your thumb and first finger (don't do this if you're pregnant) and breathe deeply.

Twenty seconds to spare

- With feet apart, breathe in deeply while you stand on your toes and clench all your muscles.
- Breathing out slowly while you sink to the floor, let everything relax.
- Don't get extra stressed if you can't balance on your toes, just do all the rest.

Half a minute to spare

- Scrunch your face into a wicked scowl.
- Relax with your mouth hanging open.
- Repeat this two or three times, then put on a smile even if you don't feel like it.
- Massage your scalp in little circles with the pads of your fingers.
- Relaxing the face and scalp keeps tension headaches at bay while the very movement of smiling sends calming signals to the brain.

One minute stress relief

- Laughter is a great stress-reliever – scan the cartoons in the newspaper or phone a telephone jokeline.
- Keep a book by your favourite funny person for when you're feeling desperate, and re-read the parts that made you laugh most.

Eat to Stay on Top

Anyone who's felt jumpy after too many coffees, or struggled to solve simple work problems after missing breakfast, knows that food affects our state of mind as well as our physical health.

UNDER STRESS, eating well is more important than ever. Vegetables, wholemeal bread, beans, dairy products and eggs, for example, provide plentiful B vitamins to build strong nerves. Stress also wears down the immune system, which is why we fall ill at difficult times – all the more reason to eat healthy food that boosts our defences.

We thrive on simple, natural foods, a wide variety of fresh vegetables, fruit, whole grains (brown bread, rice, pasta and cereals), some protein (fish, meat, dairy or vegetarian products like tofu) and some olive or vegetable oil.

You don't have to leave out all your old treats, as long as most of what you're eating comes from this healthy list. Things like bread, pasta, fruit and vegetables – complex carbohydrates – are very filling but not fattening if you don't pile on rich sauces and spreads.

Modern processed foods, on the other hand, tend to be unhealthily packed with sugar, salt, white flour,

---

Energy Foods
- Inadequate carbohydrate intake can result in fatigue and poor energy levels.
- Pasta, rice, cereals, bread, fruit and potatoes are a good source of carbohydrate energy.

---

saturated fat and artificial additives. They take the place of the nutrient-rich foods we need, and can even deplete our supplies of vitamins and minerals in trying to digest them.

A heavy meal leaves you feeling sleepy, while a high-protein supper can keep you awake. Rich foods can make you lethargic, while caffeine (in chocolate as well as tea and coffee) gives you the jitters.

Too much sugar or salt may disrupt the body's chemical and mineral balance, causing mood swings among other harmful effects. Missing a meal, especially breakfast, makes blood sugar levels fall so low that the brain can't function properly – you feel irritable and may have more accidents.

Weighty matters

If you overeat for comfort, swap to healthier treats such as fresh fruit – try a mango, a banana and a handful of cherries. Have some chocolate or chips if you want them but eat slowly, savouring the taste. Stop when you've had enough, knowing you can eat them whenever you really want to (forbidden fruit is so much more tempting). And you don't have to clear your plate or finish unwanted leftovers. Throw them to the birds.

Beware of not eating enough, though. Most slimming diets lack essential nutrients and keep blood-sugar levels low.

Dieters gain poorer scores in intelligence tests. Fortunately, the best diet for long-term weight-loss is also the best for vibrant health and serenity – low in fat, high in fresh vegetables and unprocessed foods.

Speed traps

Take a short break while you eat, even if it's only ten minutes, taking time to chew your food properly and enjoy it. Eating in a rush can trigger the release of stress hormones as well as causing indigestion. For a healthy snack, nibble some nuts and raisins, fresh

---

Super Stress-Busters
- Bananas
- Mackerel
- Marmite (brewer's yeast)
- Chillis
- Citrus fruit
- Wholemeal bread
- Oats
- Brazil nuts
- Lettuce
- Leafy green vegetables

fruit, wholemeal sandwiches with salad or a bowl of good breakfast cereal like Weetabix, Corn Flakes or low-sugar muesli.

Organize to Avoid Stress

This is for everyone who says 'I haven't got time to relax'. One of the best pieces of advice I've ever read was in a women's magazine years ago. It said, 'If you never put things down but always put them away, you'll never have to tidy up again.' How true that is – and it comes back to haunt me every time I'm 'too busy' to put things away as I go along.

FAST FOOD MAY SEEM handy when you're too busy to prepare fresh vegetables and eat properly, but, as your energy levels sink and you start catching endless infections, you lose all the time you gained, and more besides.

Being organized is the best way of making extra time in your life and cutting down stress. Admittedly, anyone with children, a home and a job may feel she's doing all the organizing a human being can possibly do. Yet there's frequently room to make things easier for ourselves. When you've done things in a certain way for years, you can sometimes get a blind spot about doing them any other way.

If you know someone who seems to be less over-worked (and not because she married a millionaire) why not ask how she does it? Share tips with your friends, you will all have different ideas. Think what a wealth of experience you've got, so have other people, and you may be able to use it. Professional organizer Denise Katz has five golden rules:

- Do it now.
- Be prepared.
- Work at your own pace.
- Don't aim for perfection.
- Sort out your priorities.

Be On Time

If you are juggling a job and a family, there is nothing worse than arriving late for work. Throughout the day, you never catch up on yourself, and end up going home late as well. It irritates both your work colleagues and your family, so make an early start, be punctual, and then you will have time to enjoy your family when you get home.

Time to reorganize

One thing I'm not suggesting is that you reorganize your day to find time for a dozen more things. If it's already hectic, which is why you're reading a book on stress relief, please don't add any extra commitments. It's better to look at all the things you're already doing and ask if you could leave any of them out.

If you don't work for the pure love of it, could you afford to work shorter hours, and use the extra time more enjoyably doing cheaper things? Could you join a bartering scheme, for example, or perhaps grow some of your own food?

Ask yourself if anything you're doing will seem like a waste of time when you look back on it in a year. And above all, don't feel guilty.

Time for you

Everyone needs time to relax and recover from the stresses of the day. So don't feel bad about spending time on yourself.

Spend some time doing the things you want to do and then return refreshed and revived to deal with the demands of the day.

Put your skills to work so you can reorganize your routine to save valuable time.

Schedule a time for relaxation, even if it's only fifteen minutes after the children are in bed and before you start clearing up.

- Promise yourself (and tell everyone) you're not going to think of anyone else in the time you have set yourself.
- Setting a timer will save you worrying you'll fall asleep. Have a quick check that nothing catastrophic is likely to happen – more to stop you leaping up with a cry of 'Have I left the gas on?' than anything else – then unplug the phone and begin.
- Swap childcare/relaxation time with a friend. Or practise some of the techniques together – as with exercise, friends can encourage each other.
- Make time to pamper yourself.

A Safe Place to Relax

Ideally, we'd all have a room we could lock ourselves away in whenever we needed some time to ourselves. An uncluttered spot that's used for nothing else, so it always has a peaceful atmosphere. Small is fine – determined relaxers have emptied boxrooms, taken over a second bathroom or put an oil heater in the shed.

FOR MOST OF US, it's a question of finding a quiet spot to call our own. A corner of the bedroom is the likeliest place, as privacy is important – you won't want an audience for your face or voice exercises. Make sure everyone knows it's your place to relax – they're not to interrupt you while you're there or pile washing on your chair when you're not.

Try to find a spot that's not associated with any other activity. You want to establish this as the place where you relax.

We are creatures of habit so, once you've used this place several times, you'll find you start to relax as soon as you sit down there. Here's what you need:

- A wooden chair, unless you're very used to sitting straight-backed on the floor – as in yoga.
- Space to stretch out on your back.

- A table, mantelpiece or bookshelf to burn candles and keep any other equipment on.
- A pile of candles, a candlestick and a box of matches.
- An oil burner and a few of your favourite scented oils.
- A cassette player and relaxing music or meditation tapes.
- Surroundings as uncluttered as possible.
- A picture of peaceful scenery, such as woodland or the sea. Instead of displaying it permanently, you could also make putting up your poster or painting part of your relaxation ritual.

Your inner refuge

My relaxation room is painted in pale colours, with a big window, filmy curtains, deep carpet, a tranquil painting on the wall and a few inspiring objects: statues, crystals and candles. There's a small indoor fountain too, and a Persian rug to lie on. Though it's upstairs, overlooking wooded hills, I can step out whenever I like into a well kept garden where roses bloom all year. Needless to say it's rent-free and never needs dusting, since it exists only in my head.

Whatever the limitations on our physical space, this is the sort of place we can all have – an inner refuge. When I close my eyes to relax I can be sitting in this peaceful room, or in dappled light under a tree, or on a riverbank or sea shore. Daydreaming? No, using a time-honoured method of restoring my mental health in a hectic day.

- Imagine a room or outdoor scene where you feel perfectly at peace. Use a picture from a magazine or make it up yourself, but visualize all the details. What's the pattern on the curtains? What flowers are there? How does the grass feel under your feet? When you're tired and stressed, imagine yourself resting there.

Breathe Your Troubles Away

One of the simplest ways of relieving tension is by breathing well – which most of us don't do. Put one hand on your chest and the other on your navel – if the lower hand doesn't move, you're not breathing deeply enough. Forget about flattening your stomach and let in a good deep breath. As you take a deep breath, feel the abdomen rise and see the movement parting your fingertips.

WHILE SHALLOW BREATHING produces the stress hormone adrenaline, a deep breath puts masses of oxygen into the bloodstream for an instant health boost to the whole body. No wonder it clears our heads, it's feeding our brains. Simply learning to breathe fully is a powerful way of relieving stress. Keep checking during the day till you do it constantly, not too deeply, but in a natural rhythm.

- Don't overdo the oxygen – you can have too much of a good thing. If you're feeling light-headed, either from breathing too deeply or from gulping in air under stress, breathe in and out of a paper bag a few times to restore the balance of oxygen and carbon dioxide.
- Check with your doctor before doing breathing exercises if you have epilepsy or high blood pressure.

Breathing fully

Find a quiet spot to sit comfortably, with your back straight. It doesn't matter if you sit cross-legged, with or without your back resting against the wall, or on a straight-backed chair with feet flat on the floor.

- If you're breathing fast, give yourself a minute to let it slow down naturally. Then put your hands side by side on your abdomen, fingertips meeting at or just below the navel.
- Take a deep breath through your nose and feel the oxygen pouring into every corner of your lungs. Feel the abdomen rise and watch the movement parting your fingertips. Breathe out and do it again, this time feeling your chest expand as well. Stop taking deep breaths and let your natural rhythm establish itself.
- Don't worry if it's not happening. If you're very used to holding your tummy in, you may need to push it out deliberately. The very act of making space there will let more air in.

Love Breathing

Breathing deeply and calmly, say silently to yourself 'I breathe in peace' on the inbreath and 'I breathe out love' on the outbreath. If you're worried about someone, imagine this protective cloud of love enveloping them.

HA Breathing

- Breathe in deeply through your nose, bringing your shoulders back to open your chest.
- Breathe out through your mouth with a long 'hhhhh' or 'haaaa' noise like a deep sigh, letting your shoulders relax and drop down. Try to make the outbreath longer than the inbreath.
- Repeat two or three times.
- Finish by relaxing for a moment with your eyes shut as you let your normal breathing pattern return.
- A variation of this works wonders if you're feeling so tense that you can't stop holding your breath. Simply puff all your breath out as far and as fast as you can, with a sharp 'ha!'. Then let a fresh breath in slowly to fill the space.

Single nostril breathing

- Breathe through one nostril at a time, keeping the other one covered.
- Breathe fully but not unnaturally slowly or deeply.
- After about a minute change to the other nostril.
- If you find this exercise difficult, try Ha Breathing.

Alternate nostril breathing

- Cover your left nostril with one finger and breathe in through the right while you count four seconds.
- Close both nostrils and count to two while you

hold your breath. (Leave out this step if you have high blood pressure).

- Uncover your left nostril and breathe out to the count of four.
- Keep both nostrils closed for two seconds with your lungs empty.
- Uncover your left nostril again and breathe in through it while you count four seconds again.
- Close both nostrils for two seconds.
- Cover left nostril and breathe out through the right for four seconds.
- Repeat this whole cycle three more times, then cover the right nostril.

Taking it from the Top

One of the first places stress makes itself felt is in our neck and shoulders. The face and spine also carry more than their share. How many times have you gritted your teeth, felt the weight of the world on your shoulders or found something a pain in the neck? People didn't pull those expressions out of the air – they're what really happens.

WHEN A MOMENT of stress passes we rarely leap or roll on the floor with joy, letting the tension out again. It just stays and builds up, contributing to migraine, repetitive strain injury, toothache and back pain.

Try a few easy exercises, particularly good for office workers or anyone who spends a lot of time sitting and using their hands. You can do them sitting down, but all the better if you can seize the chance to get up and move around a bit. Repeat all except the first and the last two exercises five times.

- Rub your hands together to warm them, then cup them over your eyes for a minute.
- Lift your shoulders to your ears, keep them there for a moment, then let them drop. (Be careful to look ahead as you do this or you could get a

horrible crick in the neck.)

- Look slowly from side to side, turning your head to look over your left shoulder and then your right.
- Let your head fall gently forward, bringing your chin as near your chest as possible. Slowly swing it in a U-shape, bringing your chin to your left shoulder, down again and to the right. Be careful not to go further than the shoulder or let your head tip directly backwards.
- Stretch your arms as high above your head as you can reach.
- With arms hanging down, lift your shoulders up, backwards and continuing in a circle.
- Stretch your arms out in front of you like a sleep walker, clench your fists, then quickly open them, stretching your fingers out. Flash them open and shut ten times.
- Standing up, give your hair a good shake for a few seconds. Shake your hands, then your arms and finally each leg. Run on the spot, shaking your arms till you've shaken all the knots out.

Funny face

Nobody looking? Give your face a much needed treat – it holds a lot of tension too.

- Open your eyes and mouth as wide as they'll go. Stick your tongue out and try to touch your nose.
- Purse your lips and push them forward, then stretch your mouth into a grin.
- Roll your eyes a few times. Raise your eyebrows

into your hairline, then bring them down as far as you can and grimace.

- Try wiggling your ears! A welcome side-effect of exercising the facial muscles might be to keep wrinkles at bay.

Foot-to-Head Relaxation

The most effective way to relax the whole body starts by deliberately tightening the muscles before releasing them, then focusing on the feeling of tension draining away. This can take from five minutes to as long as you like.

YOU'LL NEED A RUG to lie on. Using the same one in the same place each time helps to build up the relaxation habit. Turn up the heating, or put a blanket over you. If you wish, put on a tape of peaceful music without a strong rhythm.

- Lie on your back on the floor with feet apart and arms slightly away from the body, palms up. Close your eyes and let your breathing slow down.
- Breathe out before you tense each part of your body. Breathe naturally as you lie and feel the relaxation before tensing the next part.
- Starting with the left foot, clench your toes, flex the foot with toes upwards and try to tighten every muscle in the foot, lifting it slightly off the floor. Hold this for a few seconds, then relax, letting the foot roll naturally outwards. Feel tension pour out like a liquid soaking through the floor and away. Pause for a moment after relaxing each part of the body to feel this release of tension.

- Tighten the calf muscles. Hold this for a few seconds, then relax the calf. Tighten the thigh muscles, feeling tension around the knee as well as the thigh. Hold this for a few seconds, then relax. Feel the relaxation in your whole leg and foot. Now work up the right leg in the same way.

- Work your way up the body – buttocks, abdominal muscles, chest and finally upper back, pushing shoulder blades together before releasing them.

- The arms follow the same pattern as the legs. Clench the left fist tightly before releasing, then flex the left arm like a body-builder and relax it, then press the whole arm tightly to the body, tensing the shoulder, and release. Do the same with the right arm, clenching the fists and tensing all the muscles before releasing.

- Lift the shoulders and tense the neck as tightly as you can, raising the head slightly, then release.

- Clench the teeth, tightly close the eyes and knot up every muscle in the face. Relax with lips slightly parted.

- Feel how heavy your head is, sinking into the floor, your whole body perfectly comfortable. Lie peacefully for a few minutes, letting the relaxation spread into every cell of your body.

- Then roll onto your side and get up slowly. Stretch your arms high above your head and bring them gently down to your sides as you say to yourself 'I am calm'.

Safe and Simple
You can also work your way round the body just focusing on each part for a few moments, relaxing it and concentrating on feeling the tension drain away. This is a safer method if you suffer from high blood pressure (make extra-sure you don't hold your breath) or if you have injuries or health problems that make it painful to tense the muscles.

Make Your Own Relaxation Tape

*It's often quite hard to concentrate on working your
way round your body, especially when you're tired.
Lying down, it's easy to doze off. Hearing a voice brings
you back to what you're doing. And much as you may
need a nap, you'll probably feel better if you stick with
the relaxation.*

THIS IS ALMOST like self-hypnosis, but it is perfectly
safe. There's a huge variety of relaxation tapes on
the market. But you may prefer to hear your own voice
with your own choice of background sounds. Bear in
mind that if you use recorded background music, say
from another tape, legally you may need to pay for
permission from the copyright owners, particularly if
it could be said to be for public performance.

Decide what length of tape to buy. The foot-to-
head relaxation should take at least ten minutes –
remember you're leaving pauses to feel the muscles
losing their tension – and you can leave as long as
you want at the end to lie and rest.

If you are not using background music throughout,
you can end the tape with five minutes relaxing
music or nature sounds to bring yourself gently back
to wakefulness.

On the other side you can record the same text, perhaps with different music, and add the self-hypnosis exercise (see page 123) or instructions for other exercises from this book.

Start with a sound check to make sure you can hear your voice clearly and the music, if any, is at the right level.

Make sure you're not going to be interrupted or have distracting background noises.

You will need a stopwatch beside you to time the pauses. As you make your recording, press the 'pause' button rather than stopping if you need to take a break. But don't forget to leave the tape running while you leave the deliberate pauses! Write the name of the exercise and the time it takes to run on the label.

The script

Time yourself to see how long you want to make the pauses, then write a full script before you start, something like this:

- 'Breathe out. Flex your left foot and curl your toes up tightly. Hold that tightness. [*Pause for five seconds.*]
- 'Uncurl your toes, release the tension and let the foot fall naturally to the side. Feel the tension draining away, pouring out of your foot, while you breathe naturally. [*Pause for 10 seconds.*]
- 'Your foot is perfectly relaxed. [*Pause for five seconds.*]
- 'Breathe out. Tighten your left calf muscles and feel the tension. [*Pause for five seconds.*]

- 'Release and feel the tension draining away.'
  [Pause for 10 seconds.]
  And so on.

  Some people prefer to say, 'I'm breathing out now. I'm flexing my left foot and curling my toes' and so on.

  We take our bodies very much for granted, so you may want to add some appreciation as you go along, saying something like this:

- 'Breathe out. Focus on your left foot, which carries all the weight of your body without complaining. Flex the left foot . . .

  'Your legs carry you wherever you want to go.

  'Your buttocks are always slightly tensed to hold your spine upright.

  'Abdominal muscles protect your inner organs.

  'Chest muscles help you breathe.

  'Your spine keeps you standing tall.

  'Hands and arms are always busy on your behalf.

  'Your neck and shoulders hold your head up.

  'And your head leads your whole body.'

Massage – the Healing Touch

Massage is one of the oldest forms of healing. It's long been used to break down muscle spasm, improve circulation and help wounds heal. In fact our first instinct, when hurt, is to rub the painful spot.

A FULL BODY MASSAGE by a qualified therapist is a treat. But the basic rubbing and kneading moves are simple enough to learn in a short course or from a book. Get your partner or a friend to learn with you, so that you can practise on each other. The moves described here are just a small sample, you can make up more.

All you need are two big towels and some oil or talc. Many shops now sell specially blended massage oil, but at a pinch any vegetable oil will do.

- Make sure the room is warm enough for the person being massaged. Set the scene and make sure they are comfortable.
- Use the pads, not the tips, of your fingers and thumbs.
- Don't press directly on the spine or joints.
- Stronger pressure forces knotted muscles to relax, but check it's not hurting.
- Never massage damaged skin, varicose veins, any

inflamed area or a new sprain.

- Check with a doctor before massaging anyone with a serious illness (including cancer), hardened arteries or ulcers.

Basic back massage

Get your partner to undress and lie face down on one of the towels, arms at his sides.

Cover him from the waist down with the other towel to keep warm, then put several drops of oil on your palm and rub your hands together.

- When your hands are warm, kneel beside your partner with one hand each side of his spine, fingers pointing to his head, and rub your hands in one long movement up to the shoulders, then round and down to cover his back with a fine layer of oil.
- Starting from the base of the spine again, rub up beside the spine using your weight to apply more pressure. Hook your hands over his shoulders and pull gently towards you. Bring your hands back down the sides.
- The third time up the spine, press into the muscles beside it with the sides of your thumbs, going up a few inches with one and then the other. Go right up the neck, then stroke out across the shoulders.
- Find the edges of the shoulder blades and massage along just under them with little thumb circles.
- Finish with several long smooth strokes straight up his back, one hand going up as the other returns.
- Get him to do the same for you!

Simple massage techniques

Any kind of firm rubbing movement will help ease muscle tension and improve circulation.

Press the muscles gently, then make small circular movements with the palm of the hand.

Run your fingers away from you with the lightest of touches of the fingernails.

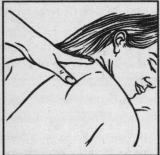

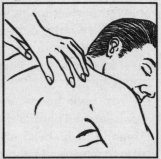

Using both hands in quick succession, pluck lightly over the fleshy areas.

Barely touching, run your fingertips lightly the whole length of the back or limb.

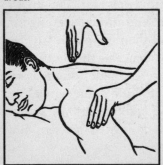

Support the head and gently grip the back of the neck to release tension.

Stroking the muscles will relax and revive. Criss-cross the movements to do both sides.

Relaxing back massage the aromatherapy way

Penny Ruth in her book *Practical Aromatherapy* tells us how we can enjoy a massage even more, and if you want to find out more about aromatherapy, turn to pp. 69–79.

When it comes to massage, you can use a single oil or mix two or three together. The best essential oils for a single-scented massage are shown below.

Best aromatic oils
- bergamot
- geranium
- lavender
- neroli
- orange
- rose
- ylang-ylang

Best therapeutic oils

- camomile (*insomnia, stress, tension*)
- mimosa (*cheering, anti-depressant*)
- peppermint (*invigorating, energizing*)
- rosemary (*mental fatigue, headache*)
- clary sage (*PMT, fatigue, depression*)
- sandalwood (*sensual, sedative, mellow*)

When it comes to combining essential oils for massage, the more scented they are the more sensual the massage will be. Touch is even more relaxing with the right aroma to refresh or restore both body and mind.

Remember, don't shower or bath for two hours after aromatherapy massage, so the essential oils have a chance to be totally absorbed.

The back is one of the best bits of the body to massage, since it has such a tangle of muscles and nerves that it responds dramatically to the right touch. It also is a large, smooth space that is ideal for spreading oil and learning strokes. Here is a selection of the best aromatherapy oils to use.

Best oils for back massage

- bergamot
- eucalyptus
- frankincense
- lavender
- orange
- petitgrain

Best combination for a relaxing massage
7 drops lavender and 4 drops each rose and mimosa in 60ml (2fl oz / 12 tsps) sunflower oil.

Energizing massage
6 drops bergamot, 5 drops peppermint and 2 drops of lemon in 60ml (2 fl oz / 12 tsps) sweet almond oil.

For backache
6 drops each lavender and eucalyptus and 3 drops lemon in 60ml (2 fl oz / 12 tsps) safflower oil.

For tense muscles
8 drops lavender, 5 drops petitgrain and 2 drops basil in 60ml (2 fl oz / 12 tsps) sunflower oil.

Quick neck and shoulder massage

This is one you can ask your partner to do at the end of a stressful day when you can both relax for the evening. It is just as effective done over clothes – with your friend sitting astride a chair with her back to you. Do each move several times.

- Put your forearms on her shoulders and press down.
- Pick up the top of the shoulders and knead the muscle, with fingers in front and heels of the hand behind. Continue this movement down the upper arms.
- Supporting her head with one hand, put the other on the back of her neck and pull fingers and thumb towards the centre.

- Still supporting her head, push up under the edge of her skull with the heel of your hand, working from one side to the other.
- While she leans on the back of the chair, massage her back in big circles with the heels of your hands.

Massage Yourself

There's a lot you can do for yourself to unknot aching muscles. Always press with the pads of the fingers, not the tips or nails, and use all four fingers together.

MASSAGE IS AN **excellent way to relieve aches and pains and the stress of everyday life** – and even better when you can use the basic techniques to help yourself when you really need them.

Head

Cup your face in your hands, then slide them back into your hair.

- Move them in large circles, pressing firmly enough to move the scalp over the skull rather than pulling the hair.
- Put the heels of your hands on your temples and make the same big circling moves with fingers in the hair.
- Then massage all over the scalp with little circling movements (good when you're washing your hair too).
- Don't forget to rub slowly up behind your ears and gently pull them up, down and back.

All these moves are excellent for easing headaches.

Face

- Put all eight fingers on your cheekbones, then, with the pads of your fingers, tap and massage in little circles.
- After working on one spot, lift the fingers and move to another without dragging the skin.
- Continue down the sides of the face, across the chin and upper lip, then up the cheeks and temples and across the forehead.

Abdomen

- Starting just below the navel and heading left, press with your fist in a large circle, anti-clockwise, out towards your side, down to the hip bone, across above the pelvis and back up the side.
- Repeat the circular movement a few times.

This helps relieve indigestion, but don't press if it hurts.

Hands and arms

- With your left hand facing down, put your right hand on top and grip it firmly, kneading the palm, then the fingers.
- Cup the left hand and knead the palm and joints with the right thumb.
- Hold and pull each finger in turn, then the thumb.
- Do the same for the other hand.
- Link the fingers and grip the hands together, then try to pull them apart.

- Squeeze and release all the way up one arm with the other hand.
- Run your hand up the arm, pressing with the skin between thumb and first finger.
- Do the same for the other arm.

Legs and feet

- Knead feet like the hands.
- Squeeze and rub the calf muscles like the arms, always going up towards the heart. This can help relieve puffy ankles.

Neck and shoulders

- Reach as far down your back as you can, then pull your fingers up beside the spine, pressing hard.
- Continue the pressure up to the top of the neck, then massage all over the back of the neck except on the spine.
- Massage under the ridge at the base of the skull, from beside the spine to the ear. Line up the fingers one above the other on each side of the spine at the top of the neck.
- Press left with the right hand, then right with the left hand, and continue this moving down as far as you can reach.
- Knead the large shoulder muscles with big pinches.

Shiatsu – Pressing a Point

Shiatsu, or acupressure, is a kind of acupuncture without needles. It works on the oriental belief that, like blood, the body's life force circulates.

JUST AS THE BLOOD is carried in veins and arteries, the life force – which the Chinese call *qi* (pronounced 'chee') and the Japanese call *ki* ('kee') – is believed to circulate in channels called meridians.

Stress, illness, injury or an unhealthy lifestyle can all disrupt the flow. Blocked energy is believed to cause fatigue or jumpiness as well as leading to illness, so shiatsu can be used to help people relax.

Western medical science doesn't recognize this invisible network of meridians, but Chinese and Japanese textbooks include very precise maps. These are what shiatsu practitioners work from when they press particular spots, known as acupressure points, to unblock trapped *qi* or stimulate the flow.

A weird idea? Well, like Chinese herbal medicine, it's all been written down and practised for thousands of years. You can try it at home, using steady pressure with the thumb, or a small circular massaging motion over the spot.

To be effective you have to press on exactly the

right spot, so if it doesn't work, try visiting a shiatsu therapist. Though it's not always totally painless (that blocked *qi* can take some pushing along) a trained shiatsu practitioner knows precisely where to press.

Toning up

- To strengthen *qi*, press the spot four fingerwidths below the navel.
- For general well-being, press the spot two to three fingerwidths towards the thumb from the outer end of the crease made when the elbow is bent at right angles. This also eases tired arms and legs.

Helpful points

Press or massage the following points for at least ten seconds.
- Anxiety. The little dip below the outer side of the knee, three fingerwidths down from the kneecaps.
- Exhaustion. Pinch the front top joint of your little finger, right on the joint itself. Also, press the centre of the palm or the central crease in the ball of the foot.
- Insomnia. Squeeze the ear lobes between finger and thumbs.
- Craving for a cigarette. Press hard on the 'salt cellar' bone between the collarbones for as long as you can – press down onto the bone, not into your throat.
- Racing thoughts and headaches. Massage the

natural dip at the temples, about an inch back from the outer edge of your eyes.

- Stress and headaches. The point between the eyebrows.
- Headaches. Under the ridge at the back of your skull, press into both sides at the same time.
- Eye strain. The edge of the nose beside the tear ducts.
- Backache. The middle of the crease behind the knee.
- Menopausal symptoms. The tip of the chin, right in the centre.
- Menstrual problems. A point in the middle of your forehead, three fingerwidths above the eyebrows.
- Sharp pain. Rhythmically press the centre of the upper lip. And be sure to see your doctor!
- Long-term pain. A point on the back of your hand, three fingerwidths down from the space between ring and little fingers.

Aromatherapy – Healing Scents

We don't use our sense of smell much in the modern world – maybe that's why it can have such a strong effect. Yet aromatic oils have been used in healing for thousands of years. More recently our grandmothers inhaled eucalyptus to cure colds and massaged their temples with lavender to ease headaches. These days aromatherapists generally use essential oils as part of a healing massage.

SCIENTISTS HAVE NOW started discovering how different scents affect the brain. Medical tests measuring brain activity have found lavender helps people relax, for example, while jasmine makes them more alert.

You can use them alone or make up your own recipes. Don't worry if one you find soothing is described somewhere else as 'stimulating' – some, like rose and neroli, may stimulate the brain but soothe the nerves at the same time. Others balance the emotions, calming or stimulating as needed – these include geranium, rosewood and valerian.

Your favourite and most effective fragrances can be incorporated into your everyday beauty routine.

Essential oils

Essential oils give the aroma of the plant but they also contain dozens of helpful complex chemicals. The main rule when it comes to buying essential oils is to be led by your nose. Since our sense of smell is so closely linked to our memories and feelings about each aroma, it is a very personal thing.

On your first buying trip, do not try to sniff every oil in the shop. There are so many, you'll only end up being confused. The human nose tires quickly and switches off if it is bombarded with different aromas, so take a list of the ten oils you are most interested in from a therapeutic point of view and start by sniffing those and you will instinctively choose the oils which you find most appealing. These are likely to do you the most good.

Good mixers

In general, the most useful oils are those which mix well with as many other oils as possible. They also need to have the broadest range of therapeutic uses combined with the most pleasant aromas possible. Here is an ideal small collection:

To start with: *jasmine · lavender · neroli · peppermint · rose · sandalwood*

Useful extras: *camomile · eucalyptus · geranium · lemon · patchouli · ylang-ylang*

Essential safety

Essential oils can have powerful effects.

• If you're pregnant, don't use (from these lists):

cedarwood, clary, cypress, jasmine, juniper, myrrh, marjoram or valerian. Avoid camomile, geranium, lavender and rose in the first three months of pregnancy.

- If you suffer from conditions such as epilepsy or high blood pressure, consult an aromatherapist through one of the organizations listed at the back before using essential oils.
- If an oil irritates your skin – though those on these lists should all be safe – wash it off at once.

How do you know it's a real essential oil?

Ready mixed bath or burning oils are handy for everyday use. But to get the strongest effects you need unblended essential oils. These tend to be thin, strong-smelling, quick to evaporate – and more expensive than cheaper 'essential oils' which are probably already blended. Keep oils in dark glass containers, away from heat and sunlight, with caps screwed on tightly.

The fragrance families

A way to reduce the number of essential oils you choose from initially is to establish which fragrance categories you instinctively prefer.

GREEN		
basil	eucalyptus	rosemary
camomile	galbanum	spruce
clary sage	peppermint	thyme
	pine	

SPICY		
camphor	juniper	myrrh
fennel	laurel	tarragon
ginger	marjoram	tea-tree

FLORAL		
geranium	mimosa	rosewood
jasmine	neroli	violet
lavender	rose	ylang-ylang

CITRUS		
bergamot	lemongrass	mandarin
citronella	lime	orange
lemon		petitgrain

WOODY / BALSAMIC		
ambrette	cedarwood	patchouli
angelica	frankincense	sandalwood
bay	marigold	valerian
birch		yarrow

Fill your life with aromas

- Treat yourself to a massage by an aromatherapist, or swap with a friend, using techniques from the massage section. Add two or three drops of essential oil to each teaspoonful of vegetable oil such as grapeseed, sunflower, safflower or soya.
- Electric or candle-fuelled oil burners spread the scent through a room. This is also a subtle way of treating children.
- Add half a dozen drops of essential oil to bath water as you get in. It remains effective for up to 20 minutes.

Oils to ease your mind
Relaxing
Bay, benzoin, bois de rose, cajeput, calamus, calendula, camomile, caraway, carrot seed, clary sage, cypress, frankincense, geranium, hawthorn, heliotrope, jasmine, juniper, lavender, lime, marigold, marjoram, melissa, neroli, opoponax, patchouli, petitgrain, rose, rosewood, sandalwood, taget, valerian, vanilla, vetivert, violet leaf, yarrow, ylang-ylang

Remedies for shock
Camomile, cedarwood, geranium, lavender, melissa, neroli, rose

To aid sleep
Benzoin, camomile, clary sage, cypress, frankincense, geranium, jasmine, juniper, lavender, melissa, myrrh, myrtle, neroli, patchouli, rose, sandalwood, ylang-ylang

USING ESSENTIAL OILS (Index of Common Problems)

Main Properties of Oils
- ® RELAXING, CALMING
- ⓣ THERAPEUTIC
- ⓢ STIMULATING, UPLIFTING

Oil	Anxiety	Arthritis	Backache	Breathing Problems	Cellulite	Cramps	Depression	Dermatitis/Eczema/Psoriasis	Fatigue	Fluid Retention	Hangover	Headache	Herpes	Indigestion	Influenza	Insomnia	Jetlag	Menopause	Nausea	Perspiration	P.M.T.	Rheumatism	Sexual Problems	Stress	Thrush/Candida/Fungal Problems	Travel Sickness
LIME ⓢ	●		●								●										●			●		
LEMONGRASS ⓣⓢ							●		●						●					●						
LEMON ⓢ	●				●	●								●	●					●				●		
LAVENDER ⓢ®	●	●	●			●	●	●	●	●	●	●	●	●	●	●	●	●		●	●	●		●	●	●
LAUREL ⓣ®		●	●			●									●					●		●				
JUNIPER ⓣ®		●	●		●	●			●											●	●	●				●
JASMINE ®	●					●	●	●								●					●		●	●		
GINGER ⓣⓢ	●								●										●		●	●				●
GERANIUM ®ⓢ				●		●	●	●	●	●								●	●	●	●			●	●	
GALBANUM ®	●								●																	
FRANKINCENSE ®	●						●						●													
FENNEL ⓢ					●					●				●						●						
EUCALYPTUS ⓣⓢ		●	●	●		●		●				●	●		●					●						
CYPRESS ⓣ	●		●			●		●									●	●	●	●						
CITRONELLA ⓣⓢ		●																		●						
CAMOMILE (GERMAN) ®	●				●		●				●	●		●		●					●	●			●	
CEDARWOOD (ATLAS) ⓣⓢ				●	●																					
CAMPHOR (WHITE) ⓣⓢ			●																							
BIRCH (WHITE) ⓣ							●	●														●				
BERGAMOT ®ⓢ	●						●	●			●										●	●		●	●	●
BAY ⓣⓢ		●	●																							
BASIL ⓢ							●							●							●			●		
ANGELICA ⓣ®			●												●							●				
AMBRETTE SEED ®ⓢ	●	●	●					●			●			●												

USING ESSENTIAL OILS (Index of Common Problems) (cont'd)

MAIN PROPERTIES OF OILS
(R) RELAXING, CALMING
(T) THERAPEUTIC
(S) STIMULATING, UPLIFTING

Problem	MANDARIN (R)	MARIGOLD (CALENDULA) (T)	MARJORAM (T)(R)	MIMOSA (R)	MYRRH (T)(R)	NEROLI (R)	ORANGE (S)(R)	PATCHOULI (S)(R)	PEPPERMINT (S)(T)	PETITGRAIN (S)(R)	PINE (LONGLEAF) (S)	ROSE (R)	ROSEMARY (S)(T)	ROSEWOOD (R)	SAGE (CLARY) (S)(R)	SANDALWOOD (R)	SPRUCE (S)(R)	TARRAGON (T)	TEA-TREE (S)(T)	THYME (WHITE) (S)(T)	VALERIAN (T)(R)	VIOLET (S)	YARROW (T)(R)	YLANG-YLANG (R)
ANXIETY	•			•	•	•		•	•	•	•		•	•	•	•	•				•	•		•
ARTHRITIS			•							•	•		•				•							
BACKACHE			•						•		•		•		•		•							
BREATHING PROBLEMS			•		•						•		•		•	•				•				
CELLULITE								•														•		
COLDS									•		•						•		•	•		•		
DEPRESSION			•	•		•	•		•	•		•			•									
DERMATITIS / ECZEMA / PSORIASIS		•			•			•				•				•			•	•				
FATIGUE	•							•	•				•		•		•	•						
FLUID RETENTION																								
HANGOVER									•				•		•							•		
HEADACHE									•			•	•											
HERPES		•																						
INDIGESTION	•		•						•									•						
INFLUENZA			•						•		•		•				•		•	•				
INSOMNIA	•			•		•	•			•		•							•		•		•	•
JETLAG																								•
MENOPAUSE												•			•									
NAUSEA	•								•									•						
PERSPIRATION									•											•				
P.M.T.															•									
RHEUMATISM									•	•	•		•				•			•				
SEXUAL PROBLEMS						•		•				•		•		•								•
STRESS			•			•		•				•		•	•	•	•				•			•
THRUSH / CANDIDA / FUNGAL PROBLEMS					•											•			•				•	
TRAVEL SICKNESS	•								•															

MIXING ESSENTIAL OILS

	AMBRETTE SEED	ANGELICA	BASIL	BAY	BERGAMOT	BIRCH (WHITE)	CAMPHOR (WHITE)	CEDARWOOD (ATLAS)	CAMOMILE (GERMAN)	CITRONELLA	CYPRESS	EUCALYPTUS	FENNEL	FRANKINCENSE	GALBANUM	GERANIUM	GINGER	JASMINE
LIME	●		●		●		●	●		●	●			●		●		
LEMONGRASS			●							●			●		●	●		●
LEMON	●		●	●	●	●			●	●	●	●	●	●		●		●
LAVENDER	●	●	●	●	●				●	●	●	●	●	●	●	●		●
LAUREL						●					●	●					●	
JUNIPER	●		●		●	●		●	●		●	●		●	●	●		
JASMINE					●			●	●							●	●	
GINGER	●		●	●	●		●				●			●	●	●		●
GERANIUM	●	●	●		●	●		●	●		●		●	●	●	●		●
GALBANUM		●			●				●	●			●	●		●		
FRANKINCENSE		●						●	●	●			●	●		●	●	
FENNEL					●	●		●	●		●		●	●	●	●	●	
EUCALYPTUS	●	●	●	●				●	●		●		●	●		●	●	
CYPRESS			●	●	●	●	●	●	●	●		●		●	●	●		
CITRONELLA	●	●	●		●		●				●			●		●		
CAMOMILE (GERMAN)		●			●						●	●	●	●	●	●	●	●
CEDARWOOD (ATLAS)				●	●		●		●		●	●	●	●		●		●
CAMPHOR (WHITE)				●			●		●	●			●			●		
BIRCH (WHITE)				●					●		●			●		●		
BERGAMOT	●		●	●				●	●	●	●		●		●	●	●	●
BAY				●	●	●	●	●			●	●				●		
BASIL				●				●	●	●		●		●		●	●	
ANGELICA	●							●	●		●			●		●	●	
AMBRETTE SEED		●		●				●	●		●					●	●	

Oil	1	2	3	4	5	6	7	8	9	10	11	12	13	14	15	16	17	18	19	20	21	22	23	24	25	26	27	28	29	30	31	32	33
JUNIPER			•	•			•				•						•	•			•					•							
LAUREL			•					•			•						•	•		•						•							
LAVENDER	•	•	•			•		•	•		•	•	•	•	•	•	•	•	•	•	•	•		•	•								•
LEMON	•			•	•	•	•		•		•					•	•	•				•	•	•	•	•		•					•
LEMONGRASS	•										•		•				•																
LIME	•	•	•				•	•		•	•				•	•	•	•	•	•				•									•
MANDARIN		•	•	•				•			•					•	•	•						•									•
MARIGOLD (CALENDULA)	•		•		•	•	•		•	•			•	•	•		•	•	•					•									•
MARJORAM		•	•	•	•	•	•	•		•	•					•	•	•	•	•			•		•	•	•						•
MIMOSA	•		•				•				•	•					•		•													•	•
MYRRH	•		•	•	•	•	•		•	•			•	•	•		•	•	•			•										•	•
NEROLI	•	•	•	•				•			•					•	•	•	•						•							•	
ORANGE	•	•	•	•		•	•		•							•	•	•	•	•		•	•										
PATCHOULI	•	•	•	•		•		•		•			•			•	•	•	•		•								•				
PEPPERMINT		•	•	•	•	•		•	•		•					•	•			•					•						•		
PETITGRAIN	•		•	•		•		•	•		•					•	•			•			•		•			•				•	
PINE (LONGLEAF)	•		•	•				•	•							•	•		•	•													
ROSE		•				•				•				•			•	•		•								•	•				
ROSEMARY	•			•	•											•		•					•	•									
ROSEWOOD	•		•	•				•	•		•		•	•	•		•	•		•			•	•				•					•
SAGE (CLARY)		•	•													•		•		•													
SANDALWOOD	•		•	•	•				•	•			•	•	•		•		•	•			•	•				•					
SPRUCE		•								•				•				•		•													
TARRAGON		•							•	•								•		•												•	
TEA-TREE			•		•					•				•																			
THYME (WHITE)		•	•				•	•		•			•			•			•	•													•
VALERIAN		•	•						•										•												•		
VIOLET	•		•	•	•							•	•	•			•			•		•		•									•
YARROW			•						•	•							•																
YLANG-YLANG	•		•	•			•	•								•	•	•	•	•				•				•					•

MIXING ESSENTIAL OILS (cont'd)

	AMBRETTE SEED	ANGELICA	BASIL	BAY	BERGAMOT	BIRCH (WHITE)	CAMPHOR (WHITE)	CEDARWOOD (ATLAS)	CAMOMILE (GERMAN)	CITRONELLA	CYPRESS	EUCALYPTUS	FENNEL	FRANKINCENSE	GALBANUM	GERANIUM	GINGER	JASMINE
MANDARIN	●								●					●	●	●		
MARIGOLD (CALENDULA)										●	●							
MARJORAM			●		●				●				●			●	●	
MIMOSA		●		●					●					●	●	●		●
MYRRH						●						●		●				
NEROLI		●		●					●	●	●			●	●	●		
ORANGE	●		●				●							●	●	●		
PATCHOULI			●						●	●	●			●		●	●	●
PEPPERMINT	●		●		●		●	●				●	●			●		
PETITGRAIN	●		●		●								●					
PINE (LONGLEAF)	●		●		●	●	●	●				●	●		●			
ROSE		●		●					●	●	●		●		●	●	●	●
ROSEMARY	●		●	●	●			●	●	●		●	●	●		●	●	
ROSEWOOD		●			●											●	●	●
SAGE (CLARY)			●		●				●				●	●		●	●	●
SANDALWOOD				●	●				●			●	●	●		●	●	●
SPRUCE	●		●						●				●				●	
TARRAGON			●			●	●											
TEA-TREE					●			●					●			●		
THYME (WHITE)	●		●		●	●			●				●					
VALERIAN								●	●				●			●		
VIOLET		●									●					●	●	
YARROW									●					●	●	●		
YLANG-YLANG		●		●										●		●	●	●

JUNIPER
LAUREL
LAVENDER
LEMON
LEMONGRASS
LIME
MANDARIN
MARIGOLD (CALENDULA)
MARJORAM
MIMOSA
MYRRH
NEROLI
ORANGE
PATCHOULI
PEPPERMINT
PETITGRAIN
PINE (LONGLEAF)
ROSE
ROSEMARY
ROSEWOOD
SAGE (CLARY)
SANDALWOOD
SPRUCE
TARRAGON
TEA-TREE
THYME (WHITE)
VALERIAN
VIOLET
YARROW
YLANG-YLANG

Reflexology – Body and Sole

The idea behind reflexology is that the whole body is represented in the foot, so pressing a certain part of the sole has an effect on the corresponding part of the body. Some people claim the same is true of the hands and even of the ear lobes.

REFLEXOLOGISTS SAY while massaging the foot, if there's something wrong with the part of the body that that spot represents they find a crunchy feeling like grains under their fingers – so they press harder to break it down. This way, they can safely tackle spinal injuries or internal organs, though a professional reflexology session may be quite uncomfortable in places.

It's been proved effective in treating premenstrual tension, and not only because any kind of massage makes people feel better – it was tested against an ordinary foot massage. Some hospitals now offer it to patients after surgery.

Relax and revive

Run your finger along the ball of your foot, furthest from the toes, and you'll find a natural curve as if two sections were joined. Find the spot in that curve just below the ball of the foot and nearly halfway across from the inner edge, and keep pressing with your thumb to massage the solar plexus point.

Headaches

Squeeze all over the pad of the big toe – this is also said to stimulate the brain. If a headache is caused by sinuses, squeeze the sides and back of each toe. A tired headache across the forehead can be eased by pressing just below the big toenail.

PMT

The womb point is halfway between the bottom of the inside ankle bone and the point of the heel. The ovaries are in the same spot on the outside of the foot and the fallopian tubes are represented by a line running across the top of the foot joining the ankle bones. You could also press the pituitary gland spot, at the bottom of the big toe pad, right in the middle.

Sore breasts

Gently rub up and down the top of the foot, covering a couple of inches from the base of the toes.

Aching shoulders

Holding the foot in both hands, knead and massage

your way across both top and sole about an inch from the toes.

Backache

The big toe represents your head, so the spine runs all the way down the inside edge of the foot. Pressing and kneading all the way down could ease tired back muscles.

Reflexology – Hitting the spot

Anyone can do a wonderfully relaxing foot massage, rubbing and kneading with a little cream or oil and pulling the toes. Just press firmly enough not to tickle! A professional will do the best job – but here are some points to try.

- Hold the foot firmly, and press your thumbs into any point that needs massaging. You can also massage in small circular movements.
- Use the rounded pads of your fingers or thumbs above the top joint (short nails are best).
- Don't massage over broken skin or injuries.

The Alexander Technique

Remember, as a child, being prodded in the back and told to stand up straight? Yet standing up straight, to most adults, means lifting the chin, throwing the shoulders back and the spine forward at the waist – a rigid, unnatural posture. The rest of the time, we slouch. Either way, we're putting a cruel strain on the spine – which has enough to contend with trying to keep us upright.

THE ALEXANDER TECHNIQUE IS named after a young Australian actor who, at the turn of the century, found his voice becoming weak and hoarse. Doctors couldn't help, and resting only worked till he went back on stage. Finally he realized his tense, stiff-backed posture was crushing his vocal cords – and damaging his whole body. Starting by curing his own problem, he worked out a series of exercises to break the bad habits of a lifetime.

It sounds like hard work, but it's actually about making movement easier. For most of us, the way we stand and move now is a lot more effort than it should be. Our backs ache, our shoulders knot up with tension.

Getting up from a seat, we tip our heads back or push off with our hands instead of letting the powerful leg muscles lift us forward in one easy, fluid movement.

We stand with the pelvis tipped forward, one leg taking the weight, one shoulder leading – it seems natural simply because we've grown used to it, but it takes far more effort than is necessary. But once you've learned the easy way to do things, you may wonder how you could have made all that effort every day.

There are books on the subject, but it's really worth taking one-to-one tuition or, more economically, group classes. A teacher can correct oddities that you were not aware of.

Let the tension run out

- Lie on your back on a carpeted floor, with a pile of paperback books beside you.
- Put the books under your head, experimenting till your neck is straight rather than tipped back (as it would be without any support) or forward. This usually takes more books than you'd think – a pile anything up to four or five inches high, depending on how rounded your shoulders are. As your posture improves, you won't need so many.
- Raise your knees slightly so the small of the back sinks naturally to the floor. Gently bring one knee at a time up to your chest for ten seconds, then shuffle your bottom further along the floor to lengthen the spine. With feet on the floor, shoulder-width apart, keep the knees comfortably raised.

How to get up from a seat

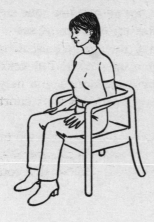

Hands off the chair arms — so you are not hunching your shoulders.

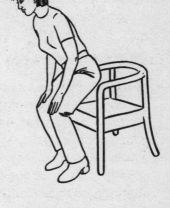

Allow your powerful leg muscles to take the strain. It's what they're for!

Keep your spine straight with head and neck aligned at all times. Do not throw your head up or backwards.

- You may find it easiest to rest your toes against a wall to stop them sliding. Rest your hands on your lower abdomen and relax for at least ten minutes. Get up by rolling onto your side, then your knees.
- Sometimes this may make the lower back ache temporarily, but don't give up – it's the muscles starting to let go of long-held tension.

Yoga – Your Flexible Friend

It's not just about strange postures and enviably supple spines. Yoga is now credited with relieving a host of diseases and it's probably the most popular form of exercise for relaxation.

YOGA DOES MORE than just improve flexibility, important though that is – it is believed to have an effect on the hormones and, by emphasizing correct breathing, improves the oxygen supply to the whole body. Most classes include breathing exercises and relaxation as well as the asanas or poses.

Like meditation, yoga is sometimes mistaken for some kind of cult. Wrong in both cases – religions may use these techniques, just as Christian churchgoers sing and eat bread – but they're also just healthy things to do.

Smart moves

Yoga can be strenuous, especially if you're stiff or unfit, and some postures put a lot of pressure on joints or the spine.

If you have back problems or find ordinary yoga too demanding, look for specialist classes, which often have names like 'yoga therapy'. Some organizations train instructors in the use of yoga to treat physical problems – not only back pain but diseases like asthma and multiple sclerosis.

Easy yoga postures

The help of a good teacher is important, as it's often difficult to tell if your position is slightly out of line. But these simple asanas can help with tiredness, backache and stress.

The Inverted Corpse

Never mind the name – it's wonderful when you're tired. If anyone asks, it's your yoga homework. Just lie on your back near a wall and rest your feet a short distance up the wall, legs together. It's good for varicose veins too, but don't do it if you have high blood pressure.

The Pose of a Child

Very restful, especially for a tired back. Kneeling on your heels, lean forward as far as you can and place your forehead on the floor. Rest your face on a cushion if you can't reach the floor. Let your arms lie beside your legs, palms up. Stay as long as you like, breathing normally.

The Butterfly

Performed as a warm-up exercise for the Lotus position, the Butterfly begins with spine erect and soles of the feet together, close to the body.

Carefully lean forward, clasping the feet with both hands. Keep movements slow and breathing steady. Lotus warm-up exercises increase hip, knee and ankle flexibility.

Lean forward gently, do not over stretch to begin with. Sit up, clasp the feet, move the knees up and down like the wings of a butterfly then press the knees to the floor.

The Mountain

Sitting, preferably with legs crossed in front of you, inhale and raise your arms above your head, close to your ears, palms together. Stretch upwards for as long as it feels comfortable, breathing naturally. Breathe out as you bring them down.

The Harmless Cobra

The Cobra usually involves coming up onto your hands and arching your spine with your head tipped back. The harmless cobra is a more spine-friendly version. Lying on your front with your face on the floor, put your elbows on the floor beside you at shoulder-level, fingers pointing forwards. Lift your head and come smoothly up onto your elbows, facing ahead. Push your ribs forward to feel the stretch in your spine.

The Harmless Cobra

Safety First
- Yoga can reduce high blood pressure but certain postures could be dangerous – see your doctor first.
- It's best on an empty stomach.
- Avoid head and neck stands if you have back trouble.
- Don't stay in a position if it hurts.
- Tell your teacher if you have a medical condition.
- Avoid anything that feels dangerous.

T'ai Chi – Chinese Serenity

*Have you ever seen pictures of hundreds of people prac-
tising slow, ballet-like exercises together in a Chinese
park as the sun comes up through the mist? You can still
see this any morning in towns and cities across that vast
country. They're doing t'ai chi (or tai ji quan), probably
the most peaceful, graceful form of exercise ever invented.*

T'AI CHI IS A FORM for spiritual meditation, working
on the principles of the constant flow of movement. Surprisingly, t'ai chi started out as a martial art!
Developed more than 400 years ago, this calming technique now forms part of Chinese astronauts' training.
According to traditional theory, t'ai chi tackles illness
by balancing the *qi* – the body's energy or life force.

To a westerner, the most obvious benefits are in
lowering blood pressure, relieving chest disease,
improving flexibility and bringing a profound sense
of tranquillity.

T'ai chi is so pleasing that you don't need huge
motivation to practise – it's very satisfying when you
can glide through the whole sequence, or even a
section. The only thing you need is a bit of space. The
sequence covers several yards, which is one reason
why people practise outdoors.

If you haven't quite got the nerve to glide across the local park, don't be put off. Just use the longest space you can find, adding a neat turn whenever you reach a wall. If your home's the right shape, you could leave doors open and work your way out of the living room, down the hall and into the kitchen.

Less strenuous than yoga, t'ai chi can be done by practically anyone. Even in a wheelchair you could do the upper body movements. As weight-bearing exercise, it helps keep the brittle-bone disease osteoporosis at bay after the menopause.

There are several styles, taking from five to twenty-five minutes, and some are practised with bent legs. If this is hard on your knees try one of the others or simply continue without bending so deeply – it's not vital.

Balancing the *qi*

- It's best to learn t'ai chi in a class or from a video, though there are some useful books as back-up.
- In these preparatory exercises, you start by standing with knees comfortably loose and back straight.
- Always breathe fully, into your abdomen, in time with the movements.
- Stand in a relaxed stance, transferring weight from one foot to the other whilst breathing in rhythm.

T'ai chi rod

- Focus on your 'centre', the point just below your navel.

- Hold a 12-inch ruler between your palms in front of your abdomen, parallel to the ground.
- Slowly move it a few inches up, out, down and back towards you, making smooth circles.
- You can also do this while walking, one circle for each step.

Qi gong march, bouncing ball

- As you breathe in, bend the right elbow and slowly lift the hand, keeping the wrist loose and palm down, to shoulder-level.
- Raise the opposite knee at the same time. Look straight ahead.
- As you breathe out, bring down the hand as if bouncing a ball in slow motion, and bring down the foot at the same time.
- Breathe in, raising the other hand and foot.
- Repeat ten times or more, until you are tired.

Exercise – Dump Your Stress

It's something most of us feel guilty about not doing enough of. Yet working up a sweat is a guaranteed route to relaxation. Aerobic exercise – that's anything that speeds up your heartbeat, not necessarily an aerobics class – increases the brain's output of endorphins, which give a natural high.

L IVELY EXERCISE improves whatever mood you're in – if you're depressed it'll cheer you up, and if you're fine it'll leave you feeling dynamic. It also works off harmful stress hormones. And the fitter you get through regular exercise, the better your body can cope with stress.

Exercise may at first seem just like hard work, but you'll soon find that it can be good fun at the same time as being good for you!

Gentle methods based on increasing flexibility help in a different way, calming and lowering blood pressure. If you're out of shape, start slowly with a daily walk. If you are new to exercise classes, choose an activity where you can work out at your own pace, or start off at home with a video. You can always wear an unrevealing tracksuit if you progress to fitness classes – anyway, everyone else is too concerned about their own shape to notice yours!

See what's on at local sports and leisure centres, gyms, colleges and evening classes, then choose something you enjoy at a level that's not too hard (if you're constantly struggling, you're more likely to injure yourself or give up). If you fancy aerobics but don't enjoy one class, try someone else's. Look out for unusual activities, like circus skills or ethnic dance classes that sound like fun.

What's your style?

Think what you'd enjoy most, and what you don't want. Swimming's out, for example, if you need something you can do in odd spare minutes. If you're not likely to be free at the same time every week, avoid new skills you have to learn in a class. If you need to be highly controlled and organized in your everyday life, give yoga a miss and go dancing.

Do you want

Activities with music?

Dancing, aerobics and a wealth of other fitness classes are now available, such as sliding, stepping and spinning (group exercise-biking).

To make friends?

Try rowing, team sports, and there's a possibility with any classes, of course. With team games, you'll need to make a regular commitment to your fellow team mates.

Playing safe

High-impact aerobics (with running or jumping moves) should always be done in a gym with a purpose-built sprung floor. Exercise instructors should have formal qualifications and they'll know the latest about safe and effective exercises. Let the instructor know if you have any health problems.

• To find good, safe videos, read the reviews in health and fitness magazines.

• If you suffer from any illness, especially high blood pressure, you should see your doctor before taking up exercise.

Something you can do alone?

Running, power-walking, skipping, exercise-biking, skating, cycling, swimming, exercise videos are all possibles. If you get bored, or feel a lack of encouragement, join a club or work out with a friend.

A new skill?

For martial arts, dance, fencing, gymnastics, acrobatics, you'll need perseverance – and be willing to take a few falls.

Outdoor activities?

In canoeing, climbing, rambling, orienteering, skiing, you can get cold, wet and possibly hurt, but never bored.

Something not too strenuous?
Try circle dancing, swimming, T'ai chi, Yoga and similar gentle movement classes.

Something demanding?
Try boxing workouts, martial arts, some team games, outdoor activities (some leisure centres also have indoor climbing walls), advanced fitness classes.

Partner activities?
Get a friend to join you for tennis, table tennis, badminton, squash. Best if you're at similar levels.

Stretch – Relax Like a Cat

❈

One of the first ways stress shows itself in our bodies is through stiff, knotted muscles that eventually stop us moving freely. Stretching is a simple way to release the tension. It's a good way to start the morning or to follow a foot-to-head relaxation and is valuable before and after exercise. Just watch a cat or dog enjoying a long, all-body stretch – tension never gets a look-in.

WHEN YOU'RE STRETCHING, never make fast or jerky movements, bounce, or try to force a stretch too far. You can stretch more by breathing out as you make the effort, breathing in and then gently leaning a little further into it as you breathe out again.

All these stretches are done standing up – straight but not stiff or arching the back – unless otherwise specified. Hold each one for five to ten seconds and repeat a few times. When you've stretched one side or limb, do the other too. You can also include some of the upper-body relaxers on pp. 47–48.

- Do some big waking-up stretches – arms up over head and out to the side as far back as they'll go, stretching out to the tips of your fingers. You can do this lying down too, stretching your legs out and down as far as they will go.

- Tilt your head sideways till your ear is near your left shoulder, then do the same the other side, then let your chin sink onto your chest.
- Stretch arms out in front, interlacing fingers and turning palms outwards. Raise above head and back as far as they comfortably go.
- Roll both shoulders backwards in big circles.
- Keeping your spine straight and hips still, put both hands on your left hip and turn your whole body from the waist to look over your left shoulder, pushing gently with your hands.
- On hands and knees, hump your back as high as you can, head down, then stretch with back straight, head level, so the spine continues in a straight line up to the skull. (Don't do this if you suffer from epilepsy.)
- Sit on the floor with legs splayed out, knees soft – don't try to push the legs down flat or lock the knees. Lean towards your right ankle, trying to keep your spine straight and leaning up out of the hips.
- Rotate and flex your feet and wiggle the toes.
- Standing on one leg, pull the other foot up to your buttocks, being extra-careful not to arch your back.
- Take a short step forward then bend your knees as if curtsying, but keeping heels on the ground.
- Standing straight with feet shoulder-width apart, relax the spine by bending forward and letting the head hang down, with legs slightly bent, arms dangling. Straighten up slowly, vertebra by vertebra, unrolling from the bottom of your spine very gradually up to the top. If you lose your

balance you can try this leaning against a wall, or with the help of a friend, but if you experience dizziness leave this exercise out.

Walk Away from Your Troubles

*Walking combines proven stress relief with the easiest,
most convenient form of exercise and the cheapest way of
getting around. Instead of short car journeys, try to take
a walk every day, even just for ten minutes – for example
in your lunch break. Or try getting off the bus a couple of
stops earlier. Most relaxing of all is a long country walk
with a picnic – and water – in your backpack.*

IT'S BEST TO WEAR lace-up walking shoes or trainers
and start with some leg stretches. But don't worry
if circumstances aren't perfect, any walk will do you
good.

- Set out at a stroll for the first five to ten minutes.
Walk tall, with shoulders relaxed and your back
straight but not stiff. Breathe deeply. If you like, try
to relax each part of your body on the way, as in
the Safe and Simple foot-to-head relaxation – 'My
left foot feels perfectly relaxed' and so on.
- Start noticing your surroundings. Enjoy front
gardens of houses. Feel the bark of trees. Really
look at the texture and colour of old brick walls.
Smell flowers. Listen to all the surrounding noises
and start distinguishing sounds – birdsong, traffic,
voices, footsteps, radios, animals.

- Speed up till you're walking briskly, breathing harder and swinging your arms. At this speed, it's good aerobic exercise.
- As you get fitter, you could combine walking with patches of jogging or pump your arms like a race-walker. You shouldn't be gasping – keep to a pace at which you could just about hold a conversation.
- Slow down to a comfortable stroll for the last five or ten minutes, to avoid cramps and slowly bring breathing and heart rate back to normal.

Walking back to happiness

Any time you feel like screaming, get out and walk fast for a few minutes till you've cooled down a bit. Help this along by breathing as deeply and slowly as you can. Put your upset out of your mind as soon as possible – concentrate on your movement and breathing. Then slow down and do the rest of the walking exercise.

Mind and body

Bring an extra dimension into your walk by silently repeating affirmations. Something like 'Every step brings me nearer to peace and contentment' or 'I'm in control of my life and at one with the world'.

Walking is a good time to meditate. Buddhists practise a 'walking meditation' in which they move very slowly, noting every part of the movement. Feel the ground under your heel and the rest of your foot coming down to join it. You may lose your balance at first!

When you're with children go at their pace, as the Chinese do. Stop to look at what interests them. It may take a little longer – though children are hard to rush anyway. But you'll arrive unstressed and, who knows, you may have had a more interesting journey.

Belly Dance – Eastern Promise

Any woman built on more generous lines than a catwalk model owes a debt of gratitude to those long-ago Middle Eastern women who entertained each other, on boring evenings in the harem, with a spot of belly dancing. Thanks to Hollywood, we've all seen how dynamic our natural curves can be when backed with some Arabian Nights music and a chiffon veil.

BELLY DANCING is such a fun form of exercise that you can now find classes in many towns, and, if you really get into it, with costume-making and performances. Belly dancing includes something most of us never get – flexibility work. Our modern way of life limits us to a tiny range of movements leading inevitably to stiffness, lower back pain and aching joints.

In fact belly dance, or Raqs Sharqi, probably started as a symbolic enactment of giving birth and kept women in good shape for the real event. Its swaying movements ease aching muscles and, when the rhythm speeds up, it's an energizing aerobic workout.

Here are some basic moves, so treat yourself to a tape of Middle Eastern music and get shimmying. Navel-rubies optional!

Dancing from the centre

Practise each movement several times, then start linking them to create a smooth continuous dance.

Pelvic tilts

Stand with feet slightly apart, back straight, knees slightly bent. Arms should be by your side, slightly bent with palms facing forwards. Arch your back, tipping your pelvis down. Then contract your buttock muscles and flatten out your lower back, thrusting forward with the pelvis.

Hip swinging

Standing with feet slightly apart, swing your hips from side to side in a straight line, trying to keep your shoulders still.

Pelvic circles

Now link the movements for pelvic tilts and hip swinging – arch your back, push your right hip out sideways, flatten your back, push the left hip out – so you've made a circle. Continue in a smooth circling movement. Vary the sizes of the circle, some small, some as large as you can without moving your shoulders.

Travelling tilts

As your pelvis thrusts forwards in a tilt, take a short step forward with the right foot. Tilt back, then do two quick thrusts. On the second one step forward on the left foot. Do two more thrusts and then step forward on the right foot.

Travelling circles

As your hip comes round to the right take a small step forward with the right foot. Complete the circle, then as the hip moves left take a small step with the left foot. Remember to leave one and a half circles between steps.

Figure of eight

Next, change the circle to a figure of eight – sideways to the right, forward, back to the left, sideways to the left, forward, back to the right. It takes a bit of practice to create a smooth movement.

Belly roll

Suck your stomach in and lift your ribcage, so your back is slightly rounded. Push your abdomen out, then in, in a continuous undulating movement.

Shimmy

With arms out beside you at shoulder level, move your shoulders backwards and forwards fast to shake your breasts.

Autogenic Training

⊗

Don't put up with stress, train your body to relax with this simple technique and enjoy instant relaxation on tap. This method of harnessing your brain's healing powers sounds very technical, but in fact autogenic training is a simple way of teaching our bodies to relax. It's a down-to-earth technique, invented by a doctor in the 1920s, and is probably the most effective relaxation method developed by a westerner. But it has surprising effects – you can actually learn to make your skin warmer or cooler at will.

AUTOGENIC TRAINING INVOLVES a series of mental exercises, telling yourself for example that your abdomen is warm and your forehead is cool. Eventually you will feel this healthy change in temperature – it has even been known to cure migraines.

Like the other techniques in this book, it's not magic or linked with anything supernatural. It's just learning to put our natural abilities to good use.

You can learn autogenic training in small groups, meeting once a week and practising at home for about two months, or from books. It takes a little will-

---

Warning
Don't try autogenic training if you suffer from epilepsy, insulin-dependent diabetes or schizophrenia, or within three months after a heart attack. If you suffer from glaucoma, make sure your condition is monitored.

---

power at first, as with anything that involves learning and repeating a technique, especially if you use a book rather than classes. But it's not at all difficult, and since you practise while sitting or lying down comfortably, you don't need a lot of energy to get started. It's also handy because you can do it at any time.

The real beauty of autogenic training is that you're programming yourself to relax at will. The idea is that, once you've drummed a suggestion like 'My head and shoulders are heavy' into your brain often enough, you'll only have to say it to feel the effect. Your muscles really will feel heavy and relaxed as they instantly let go of tension. Having put in the work at the beginning, you should then have instant relaxation on tap.

Heavy work

Buy a packet of blue sticky-paper dots from a stationer's and stick them on mirrors, windows, your watch, the kettle, your wardrobe door, equipment at work – anything you're likely to glance at during the day.

- Every time you see one of these dots, repeat 'My neck and shoulders are heavy' several times, feeling the heaviness as much as possible. The idea is to say it about 100 times a day.
- Eventually it will have a relaxing effect when you only say it once – and possibly whenever you see the colour blue! This is a very simplified version of the main technique.

Meditation

⊠

If the word 'meditation' conjures up images of hippies and bearded gurus, think again. One of the most proven forms of stress relief, it's used by top business people and prescribed by doctors. The idea is to clear your mind by concentrating on one simple, even meaningless thing, such as counting. Then the brain switches from its busy everyday mode into the 'alpha' state – relaxed, alert and effective.

MEDITATION – STILLING the mind's chatter – has been practised all over the world for thousands of years. Prayer, yoga, t'ai chi, breathing exercises, even the focusing methods that actors and athletes use – they're all forms of meditation. Think of stumbling though a toy-littered room with unwashed dishes cluttering every surface. Then see the same room clean, tidy and freshly painted. It's not a miracle, just a bit of work. Meditation has a similar effect on our minds.

You can learn it through religious and non-religious organizations, books and evening classes, including the expensive but effective Transcendental Meditation. Or simply use any of the following methods.

Monkey-mind

Meditation stills the chatter that runs through our minds like a monkey swinging from branch to branch. But 'Monkey-mind' will put up a pretty good fight. It will produce endless distractions – anything to put off its bedtime! You just have to ignore it and keep bringing your attention back to meditating.

Choose one method and promise you will do it each day for the next week. Try to meditate at the same time and in the same place every day.

- When thoughts come into your mind (as they do for everyone) just let them drift on out. Some people imagine wrapping them in a bubble and blowing them away. Calmly bring your mind back to the meditation.
- Very occasionally, meditation brings up a disturbing image. Just let it float out like any other – it's bubbled up like marsh gas and doesn't mean anything. If it bothers you, try a different technique such as mindfulness.
- Stick with it for the set time, even when it doesn't seem to be working. Meditation gets easier as you go on. And you get some benefit just from trying.

Seated meditation

Sit comfortably with your back straight. Set a timer for ten minutes – eventually you can work up to thirty – and close your eyes. Let your thoughts subside and your breathing slow down. Stay focused on what you're doing. Don't breathe so deeply that you feel dizzy.

Counting

Count 'one' at the end of your first outbreath, 'two' at the end of the second, and so on. Start again from one when you reach ten or if you drift off and lose your place.

Breath focus

Simply focus on the feel of the breath as it enters and leaves your nose. Alternatively, use any breathing exercises.

Mantra

Silently repeat a calming word or phrase with every outbreath, such as 'Peace', 'Stillness', 'Love', 'Joy', 'Yes', 'I am calm' or, if you have religious beliefs, 'God is love'. Try the Indian sacred word 'Om', which you can also say aloud on every outbreath.

Candle

Instead of closing your eyes, light a candle and look at the flame, blinking as often as you need to.

Mindfulness

※

Mindfulness – focusing on where you are – has the same good effects as seated meditation but doesn't take up any time, because you practise it while you're doing other things. Mindfulness just means focusing on what you're doing – another way of quietening the mental chatter.

MOST OF THE TIME we're only half aware of the present moment. Our minds run a constant background track of worries, daydreams, plans and memories. We mull over old arguments, giving ourselves a brilliant last word, and recall bits of last night's television. It's like a pile of junk mail in the head.

Because it's so distracting, this makes it hard to concentrate when we need to, and even when we're doing something for pleasure we're only half there.

Mindfulness is a way of training ourselves to be fully 'in the moment'. It makes work easier and good times more enjoyable. Then relaxation comes naturally.

Mindfulness at work

- When you're washing up, instead of daydreaming or wondering what to get for the next meal, just be totally, calmly aware of what you're doing. Notice the feel of your hands slipping into warm water, the creamy texture of the bubbles, the sound of plates clinking against each other. Be aware of other sounds around you, but without thinking about them.

- The same with any other everyday chores and activities – we stop being like robots when we really experience the movement of a vacuum cleaner over a carpet, the speedy clicking of a keyboard, the swaying of a bus.

Mindfulness at leisure

- Make sure you have time to sit down to a meal, then look at the food, smell it and notice how it makes you feel. Eat slowly and with pleasure, enjoying the texture as well as the taste, noting any memories or concerns that come to mind, but without dwelling on them.
- Practise mindfulness in the shower – be aware of the feel of the water on your skin.

Use it to give up smoking

If you want to give up smoking, try smoking consciously.

- Pick up the packet. Hold it between both hands, really feeling the shape and smoothness. Take out a cigarette, look at it as if you'd never seen one before, feel it in your hands and between your lips. Don't smoke while you're doing anything else, but focus on the taste, smell and feel of it right up until you slowly and mindfully stub it out. Believe it or not, this has helped many people give up.

The road to serenity

Mindfulness makes it easier to concentrate as well as preventing stress building up. After you've been practising for a while, so you're not distracted by doing things in this new frame of mind, try it when you are driving.

- Keep your attention on all the things you need to do to drive safely, looking out for pedestrians and other traffic.
- Be aware of your own movements, your hands on the wheel, your feet on the pedals, instead of worrying about the time or other people's behaviour.
- Make this the best drive you are capable of.

Moving Meditation

⚙

If you find it hard to sit and meditate, why not try moving meditation – or stillness in action, as it has been called? It's one step on from mindfulness – this time you're doing something active specifically to clear the mind.

YOU CAN REACH the relaxed, alert alpha state through all kinds of movement – dancing spontaneously or with learned steps (especially folk or circle dances), running, playing tennis. T'ai chi and yoga are forms of moving meditation.

It sometimes happens by itself when you're engrossed in an activity – when you feel the rhythm or music flowing through you as if you're part of it. You may even recognize it from times when you've been swimming or playing sports in the past.

When you're alone, try putting on some favourite music and dancing to it, not bothering about how you look but trying to follow the music, as if your body is becoming part of it. Dancing has a doubly stress-relieving effect, combining the relaxing benefits of moving and listening to music.

Experiment – try various different kinds of music, rap or classical or a folk tune – things you hadn't thought of dancing to. No need to try complicated steps. It's to let the music move your body and the movement still your mind.

Another route to moving meditation is through more formal exercise.

Energy moving

- Stand with back straight (not arched), arms by your sides. As you breathe in, raise your arms, palms up, stretching out to the fingertips as they reach above your head. Imagine yourself summoning up energy and breathing it in.
- On the outbreath turn the palms down and bring them slowly down beside you.
- Imagine breathing out your worries, and your hands bringing your stress levels down. Do this slowly at least ten times and feel stress ebbing away.

Infinity

- Move your hips in the belly dance figure-of-eight (a horizontal eight, like this, is the symbol for infinity). Then let your body sway with it, arms circling at waist height like a Hawaiian dancer, and lose yourself in this timeless movement.

Water weed

- Put on music you could move to, without vocals. Stand with feet about shoulder-width apart, knees slightly bent, hands hanging loosely.
- Imagine you're a frond of water weed, being

moved by tides and eddies. Let the water move your body in swirling motions including your arms and head, letting your knees bend.

- Flop forward from the waist and let the tide lift you up and round. Think of nothing but the water flowing around you.

Spiralling

- Sitting or kneeling with your back straight and head held high, breathe in and turn to the right, reaching out behind you with your right hand.
- Move from the hips, head and body moving as one. Stretch your arm back as far as it will comfortably go. Bring your outstretched arm up and reach for the ceiling as you face forward again.
- As you start breathing out, turn to the left and bring your arm down and across to the left thigh, in a smooth spiral motion.
- Keep breathing steadily as you repeat the movement with the left arm towards the right side.

Hypnosis – Reach Your Inner Self

❧

Say 'hypnosis' and most people will think of a melodra-
matic villain with piercing eyes, or a stage full of
revellers who all think they're Elvis. Yet its most popular
use these days is in hypnotherapy – a way of solving
problems through the power of the patient's own mind.

HYPNOTHERAPISTS ARE SETTING UP shop all over
the country, and – judging from the number of
people who say they've been helped to relax, lose
their phobias, control panic attacks or give up
smoking – it can do a lot of good.

Being hypnotized is quite a relaxing experience in
itself, but that's not its main point. It's a way of
bypassing the conscious mind so the therapist can
implant helpful suggestions such as 'I am perfectly
relaxed' or 'I easily do all my work and still have
plenty of energy' in the subconscious, which accepts
them more readily.

Why bypass the conscious mind? Because it's full
of everyday clutter and worries. If you say 'I am
relaxed' it's just as likely to retort 'No you're not, or
you wouldn't be doing this'.

Some hypnotherapists also offer psychotherapy –
which may include discovering how events from the

What Could Go Wrong?

• Hypnosis can't make you do something you'd consider totally wrong or dangerous. You might be persuaded to cluck like a chicken but not to stab someone. In rare cases male hypnotherapists have taken advantage of a client's relaxed and suggestible state, but that's abuse of trust, not mystic powers.

• Unlike a stage hypnotist, a properly trained hypnotherapist can make sure you're fully back to everyday consciousness before you leave.

• Any form of psychotherapy, with or without hypnosis, may bring up a lot of distress. So don't start unless you can afford as many sessions as it takes to sort out – and then only with someone you're sure is trustworthy and has the right professional skills. A family doctor can often make recommendations.

past still cause tension in your life, and how to get them out of your system. It's easier to do while you're in a relaxed state.

Seeing a hypnotherapist

At your first visit the hypnotherapist is likely to ask a few questions about your health and why you've come. You'll sit in a comfortable chair or lie down with your eyes closed, while the hypnotherapist talks you through a relaxation routine or invites you to imagine you're in a beautiful, peaceful place. It's not a hands-on therapy, though she may lift your arm to check if the muscles are relaxed.

Once you're deeply relaxed she'll make suggestions like 'I feel comfortable in all social situations', or whatever is relevant, and may teach you a phrase or simple technique to bring back that calm state of mind when you do it in future.

You remain conscious the whole time, probably feeling quite dreamy and very relaxed. When the therapist asks you to come out of the trance you do so at once – possibly not realizing you've actually been under hypnosis!

Many hypnotherapists will give instructions on self-hypnosis to take home, and you may only need the one session.

Self-Hypnosis

❋

Give yourself some useful new instructions. You can hypnotize yourself if you put your mind to it. It's not dangerous — you can't get 'stuck' under hypnosis or give yourself some harmful command. You'll just use the space given by deep relaxation to put some constructive thoughts where they'll do most good.

START BY LYING on the floor or sitting in a straight-backed chair, hands in your lap. If you have time, go through the foot-to-head relaxation (see pp. 50–52). If time is short, do some breathing exercises to set the scene and put you in a calm and peaceful frame of mind.

The script

Say to yourself, 'Everything I am doing makes me healthier, more relaxed, and more in control of my life. I will wake up immediately if I need to.'

When you feel comfortably relaxed, imagine sitting on a wooden bench in a beautiful garden, full of flowers. Bees are buzzing gently, and the sun warms your skin. At the end of the garden there's a gate. You walk through, noting the rough texture of the weathered wood as you push it open.

Beyond it are steps leading down to a secluded beach, with waves gently lapping on the sand. You walk slowly down, feeling the coolness of stone under your feet as you count the steps – one, two, three . . . at every step you feel more relaxed . . . four, five, six . . . deeply calm and relaxed . . . seven, eight, nine . . . your body is relaxed, your mind open to all the good that can come to you here . . . ten.

You are on this beautiful beach, knowing you are perfectly safe and can leave whenever you want. Enjoy the peace and serenity. Nearby you see a wrought-iron seat facing the sea. You sit down and say to yourself, 'I am peaceful, happy and perfectly in control of my life. I easily cope with everything that happens.'

Now pinch the fold of skin between thumb and first finger on your right hand (pinch your thumb if you're pregnant). From now on you can relax at will, simply by doing that and remembering this peaceful place.

Repeat, 'I am peaceful, happy and perfectly in control of my life. I easily cope with everything that happens. I can relax at will, simply by pinching my right hand and thinking of this place.'

When you're ready, return to the steps, knowing you can come back here any time you like. You will return to everyday consciousness as you count down, but will be able to relax at will. Count slowly down from ten, as you walk up the steps, starting to notice the everyday sounds around you. By zero you are back to everyday consciousness, relaxed and alert.

Getting started

- You can do this without making a tape, but it's easier to follow spoken instructions – simply read out the script on this page.

  Speak in a slow, calm, rather monotonous voice and remember to leave pauses. You can give yourself any suggestions you like on your secluded beach, but they must be positive, clear and harmless.

- In an emergency, just say to yourself, 'One, two three, ready.' You can snap out of hypnosis instantly, but a brief wake-up formula reduces the jolt.

- If you find it hard to visualize, just do the counting – many people find this equally effective.

- For deeper relaxation use 30 steps down to the beach instead of 10.

Sleeplessness

When you are wound up about stressful events that have occurred during the day, being unable to go to sleep is the final straw. When nothing seems to work, try this technique of self-hypnosis. It is worth learning it beforehand (read it over to yourself till you know it), then when you come to need it, it will be effortless.

- Lying down, close your eyes.
- Imagine a familiar image, say, for example, your bedroom (but keep your eyes shut). Say to yourself: 'Nothing but this room exists.'

- Visualize all the different details that go to make up this room: the ceiling, the walls (are there pictures on them?), the floor (does it have a carpet or rug?), the windows (what are the curtains like?), the furniture – dressing table, chest of drawers, wardrobe, the bed on which you are lying.
- In your mind work systematically from one end of the room to the other, from top to bottom.
- Then, one by one, wipe the image of each of these details from your mind, until everything has gone. You are left with absolute total emptiness.
- Concentrate on this void, with you in the middle of it, for a few moments.
- You will experience a feeling of relaxation coming from it.
- If you still cannot sleep, repeat the exercise several times. It's usually successful after only a few minutes of 'disconnection'.

Colour Therapy

❈

*Next time you see red, think blue – it's such a calming
colour that even the thought of it brings raised blood
pressure down. Colours affect us more than we may
think. They can change our moods. Warm ones like red,
pink, orange and yellow are stimulating, while the cool
hues – green, blue, turquoise and violet – are calming.
Blue is generally considered most relaxing. Green
promotes balance, as does dignified violet. Turquoise is
refreshing and calming.*

OUR CHOICE OF CLOTHES both reflects and rein-
forces our feelings – flamboyant, outgoing
colours, quiet neutrals, the dark shades of sadness,
bold patterns, big cheerful flowers.

For a change, try wearing blue, green or violet – as
pure and clear as possible – when you need to feel
more relaxed, balanced or confident. It doesn't have
to be head to foot – a bright silk scarf will do. If the
pure colour doesn't suit you try a different shade, or
wear it as trousers or a skirt.

The same at home – choose tranquil colours for the
bathroom and bedroom. A picture of blue sky and
green countryside is deeply soothing. Remember,
though, that walls painted in any strong colour may

be overwhelming and cold blues can be depressing. You can use the chosen colour as a highlight in bedding, towels, coloured bath oils, curtains, cushions, wallpaper patterns or anything you like to look at. White paint with a hint of colour continues the theme in an unobtrusive background.

Don't ban warm colours though, or your home could have a chilly feel. Pink and peachy shades are comforting. An all-red room would be oppressive, but it's a revitalizing colour and touches of red perk the place up.

Oh, and don't worry if teenagers shroud themselves in black, says colour therapist Susan Farrar, it's a kind of cocoon – they're coping with the death of childhood and absorbing major changes. Who knows what butterflies will emerge?

Colour visualization

Theo Gimbel recommends the effective exercises on this page in his *Book of Colour Healing*, using complementary colours for balance and well-being.

- Start by relaxing your muscles, for example with the foot-to-head technique (see pp. 50–52).
- Then lie or sit comfortably with your back straight, eyes closed, and think of yourself at a time when you were particularly well and happy.
- Keep this positive image in mind and let other thoughts drift away.
- Breathe fully into your abdomen, at a natural pace.
- As you breathe in, imagine sitting by a blue lake under a calm blue sky.

- Feel the calmness of the blue fill your body.
- On the outbreath, imagine you are looking at the intense orange of a marigold.
- Repeat this several times, then sit quietly for a while.
- You can also imagine the colour blue entering your solar plexus (just below the chest) as you breathe in, and spreading around your body beneath the skin.
- Imagine breathing out the colour orange.

Colour breathing

- For happiness and fun imagine breathing in the colour orange – breathe out blue.
- Violet increases self-respect – breathe out yellow.
- Breathe in yellow when you need to feel some detachment from things – breathe out violet.
- Green cleanses and balances – breathe out magenta.
- Breathe in magenta to let go of obsessional thoughts – breathe out green.
- Red is for vitality – breathe out turquoise.
- Turquoise strengthens the immune system – breathe out red.

Voice & Music Therapy

Stress tightens our throats (ever heard your voice come out in a squeak when you were nervous?) and, in the long term, restricts breathing without our even noticing. Using your voice not only loosens the throat – the vibration is said to benefit the whole body, like an internal massage.

SINGING IS A WONDERFUL way to relax. Oh I know, most of us are convinced we squawk like crows. But voice teachers retort, 'If you can talk you can sing,' and they're right. You may not sound like an operatic diva – but no one says that you're not allowed to run if you're below Olympic standard.

All over the world people sing to express their feelings – joy, grief, anger, spirituality, love and longing. Giving up this simple, universal pleasure is like losing the right to dance or play. No wonder so many of us suffer from tense facial muscles, causing headaches and premature wrinkles.

So let your voice dance. Sing in your bath, while you're working, with the radio, in the car or with small children – they love it. Sing scales or make up tunes with the sound 'aaa' or 'oh'.

Don't worry if your voice sounds tight or quavery,

weak or rusty – imagine what your leg muscles would be like if you hadn't used them since childhood. You'll be surprised how quickly it grows confident and strong.

The yoga lion

The yoga lion is a great exercise to loosen up your neglected facial muscles.
- Loosen up by sitting comfortably, with palms resting on your lap.
- As you breathe out, open your mouth and eyes wide and slowly stick your tongue out as far as possible.
- Splay out your fingers and look fierce, then relax as you breathe in.
- Repeat several times.

Letting it out

Screaming is a great stress-reliever. It eases tension around the face as well as relieving pent-up feelings. At night, try it in the car with the windows closed. But the best place for screaming is a funfair – choose a scary ride and shriek to your heart's content.

Reclaim your voice

Find a quiet spot where you won't worry about being overheard, then try some of these exercises, suggested by voice therapists Susan Lever and Frankie Armstrong. Don't strain to reach a note, your range will expand naturally.

- If you're tired, do some huge, exaggerated yawns to release tension around the mouth.
- If you're stressed and irritable, give some long and noisy sighs. Progress to deep groans if you feel like it.
- Humming has a soothing effect as it resonates through your body. Notice where you feel it and if it changes when you alter the note.
- Exaggerate some everyday sounds, taking a deep breath and seeing how long and varied you can make them on the outbreath. Say 'Oh!' as if you'd just heard a thrilling piece of gossip, starting at a normal level and sending your voice as high and then as low as it will go.
- Try a baffled 'Eh?' sending your voice up to the top of its pitch. Then a grumpy 'Huh', letting all the breath out in a long growly 'hhhh'. What about an 'Mmmm' going up and down the scale? And a deliciously scandalized 'Ooooh!'
- Sing pure vowel sounds on one long, strong note:
    'ah' as in 'past'
    'e' as in 'went'
    'ee' as in 'piece'
    'o' as in 'on'
    'oo' as in 'flute'.
    This can have the same effect on brainwaves as meditating.

Herbalism – Power of Plants

※

Long before scientists thought of creating drugs from plants, our ancestors used the whole plants to make a more balanced remedy. Today, a stroll through any health food shop will once again reveal herbal potions aimed at relieving stress. Where tranquillizers act like a blow with a blunt object, these have a gentler soothing effect to help the body through crises.

A HANDFUL OF RELAXING herbs tied in a cloth and hung under the hot tap makes a special bath after a hectic day.

The most popular way of taking herbal remedies, though, is as a cup of tea. Simplest of all are the many different herbal teabags now available, even in supermarkets. Look out for those produced organically, without any agricultural chemicals, and experiment to find your favourite flavours.

Some herbs have a medicinal tang and valerian has even been likened to smelly socks. But others are only lightly scented and some, like camomile and peppermint, seem to please most tastes.

Best Teas for Relaxation

Use the leaves and flowers unless otherwise stated:

Camomile flowers
Highly effective and a good nightcap.

Hops
Drink the flowers as tea, or make a traditional sleep-inducing pillow. The sedative effects are ideal if you're highly stressed, but not if you're feeling depressed.

Lavender flowers
Drink in small amounts mixed with other herbs, use in your bath or tuck a sprig into your pillow.

Lemon balm (melissa)
Put the lovely, fragrant leaves in salads or cold drinks too.

Lime flowers
Help keep blood pressure under control.

Peppermint
Alleviates indigestion, a common side-effect of stress. Ideal instead of coffee after dinner.

Skullcap
Strong and effective for all kinds of stress.

Valerian (dried root)
Don't take too much of this powerful relaxant.
Watch out too for one odd effect – some people find it makes them jumpy instead.

Wood betony
Eases stress-induced headaches.

Herbalism's Varied Uses

This table will give you some idea of the many uses herbs can have in modern-day remedies and the various ways they can be administered. If you are interested, you should read up on the subject. There a number of books available, including Christopher Hedley and Non Shaw's *Herbal Remedies* from which the following charts are taken.

HERBS	Camomile	Corn Silk	Marigold	Parsley	Peppermint	Rosemary	Sage	Thyme
Acidity	T		T					
Anxiety	T, M, B							
Arthritis				T		T, Tr, M, O	T, Tr, C, M, V	T, M
Breast Pain	C	T	T, Tr, C	T			T, Tr, C	
Colic/Flatulence	T, Tr, P, C		T		T, Tr	T, Tr		T
Constipation	T						T	
Cystitis		T		T			T, Tr, M	T+ BARLEY
Depression			T			T, Tr, B	T	
Diarrhoea	T							
Eczema	T, Tr, L, W, O		T, Tr, L, W, O	T, W	W		T	
Sore Eyes	W, C		W, C, O, T					
Fungal Infection	V		T, Tr, L, W, O					L, W, V
Headaches	T, Tr, C				C	T, Tr, C		
Insomnia	T, M, B				T			T
Menopause			T	T, Soup			T, Tr, B	
Period Pain			T, Tr	E	T			
Spots/Acne			T	P			T, Tr, W, L	

KEY: B Bath; C Compress; E Eaten; G Gargle; I Inhalant; J Juice; L Lotion; M Massage oil; O Ointment; P Poultice; Pl Plaister; S Syrup; T Tea; Tr Tincture; V Vinegar; W Wash

SPICES	Aniseed	Cardamom	Cayenne	Cinnamon	Cloves	Fennel	Ginger	Juniper
Acidity								
Anxiety						T, Tr		
Arthritis			O, M, Pl		O, M	T, Tr, M, O	O, M, B	T, O, M, B
Breast Pain						T, Tr, C		T
Colic/Flatulence	T, Tr	T, Tr		T, Tr	T, Tr	T, Tr	T, Tr	
Constipation								
Cystitis					IN HERB TEAS	T+ BARLEY		T+ BARLEY
Depression	T, Tr, M	T, Tr				T, Tr, M		
Diarrhoea				T				
Eczema								
Sore Eyes						W, C, T		
Fungal Infection					W			
Headaches		T, Tr						
Insomnia	T							
Menopause						T		
Period Pain							T, Tr, C, B	
Spots/Acne								W, L

KEY: B Bath; C Compress; E Eaten; G Gargle; I Inhalant; J Juice; L Lotion; M Massage oil; O Ointment; P Poultice; Pl Plaister; S Syrup; T Tea; Tr Tincture; V Vinegar; W Wash

Growing your own

Fresh air, exercise, useful work and feeling at one with nature – no wonder so many people love gardening. Even with a few pots on a windowsill, you can create a herb garden to supply you all year round, freshly picked or harvested at the right time of year and hung up to dry.

OTHER

	Barley	Cabbage	Carrot	Cucumber	Figs	Garlic	Honey	Lemon	Oats	Onion	Salt	Vinegar
Acidity	Water	T, J	J, Soup					IN WATER	T			IN WATER
Anxiety							IN HERB TEAS		E			
Arthritis		P, E						J	P		B	
Breast Pain		P	P									
Colic/Flatulence	Water											
Constipation		E	E		S, E				E			
Cystitis	Water							IN HERB TEAS				
Depression							IN HERB TEAS		E			
Diarrhoea			J, Soup			E		+ CARROTS			WITH SUGAR	
Eczema	W						L		W, P			
Sore Eyes				C							W	
Fungal Infection						J, O, V						W
Headaches												W, C
Insomnia							IN HERB TEAS					
Menopause									E			
Period Pain												
Spots/Acne						J		J	W, P	J		W

KEY: B Bath; C Compress; E Eaten; G Gargle; I Inhalant; J Juice; L Lotion; M Massage oil; O Ointment; P Poultice; Pl Plaister; S Syrup; T Tea; Tr Tincture; V Vinegar; W Wash

Mint, for example, grows like a weed and is often planted in containers to stop it taking over the entire garden. Skullcap, lavender, valerian, lemon balm – none of them need a green-fingered gardener. And, unlike growing flowers or veg, you can produce a useful and lovely-smelling herb garden with very little work.

Playing safe

'Natural' doesn't mean weak or harmless. In China, where traditional medicine is still taught at medical school level, herbalists prescribe concoctions with wonderdrug-like effects.

Even in Europe – where much of the herbal lore was lost after its users were branded as witches – modern practitioners have produced some startling cures. That kind of powerful brew is best made by qualified practitioners.

All the herbs recommended here can be made into a tea or 'infusion', by pouring hot water onto a teaspoonful or two and letting it brew in a teapot till it's cool enough to strain and drink.

Homeopathy – Like Cures Like

❈

Homeopathy has been in use for 200 years, longer than most drugs. But homeopathy runs on totally different principles from orthodox medicine.

HOMEOPATHY IS HOLISTIC, meaning it aims to treat the whole person rather than just curing symptoms. Its remedies are diluted so many thousand times that, according to scientists, there can't be anything of them left in the pills or drops people take. Yet homeopaths say the more the remedy is diluted, the stronger and more effective it becomes.

Its principle is 'like cures like' – a substance that causes certain symptoms can cure them if used in tiny amounts prepared in a certain way. A remedy for heart palpitations uses coffee, which can cause them, and the cure for insect stings is made from bees.

Stuff and nonsense? Oddly, it seems to work. Many reputable studies have shown that it's not just the placebo effect (people getting better because they think they will), it often has better results than conventional medicines, even when used for the treatment of animals.

Each remedy also suits a different type of person. So if you have a long-standing health problem, a homeopath will work out which of the homeopathic types you are and prescribe that remedy – to treat you rather than the disease.

For example, are you worried about a forthcoming event such as an exam? Do you set yourself high standards and fear you won't reach them? Do you crave sweet foods? Do you lie awake fretting about the past day? Do you feel better after midnight, when moving around, in cool surroundings, or after hot food or drinks? Do you feel worse in stuffy atmospheres, in the early evening and if you overeat? If so, you're a Lycopodium clavatum person! Few of us fit such a detailed picture, of course, but if most of it sounds like you that remedy could put you right.

Don't be put off trying for yourself. The more honest you can be about your character, the easier it will be to diagnose yourself from a book. And some remedies have more general first-aid uses.

To keep the remedy in its purest form, don't let it touch anything, even your fingers.

Tip tablets into the bottle top, then straight into your mouth without handling them.

Don't eat, drink, smoke or brush your teeth for at least 15 minutes before and after taking a remedy.

Insomnia

If you are feeling stress, it is quite likely that you may undergo a period of insomnia. The worst thing is to wake up at 2 or 3 a.m. night after night, for if you cannot get a good night's sleep, you will feel even less able to cope the following day.

Homeopathy provides several remedies that will

Do-it-Yourself Remedies
- *Aconitum napellus*, a first resort for fear or panic attacks and after physical trauma.
- *Anacardium* for anxiety caused by indecisiveness, possibly hidden under a tough exterior.
- *Argentum nitricum* when you're so worried you can't concentrate.
- *Arnica* for emotional or physical shock.
- *Arsenicum album* for anxiety in a perfectionist.
- *Avena sativa* for exhaustion caused by long-term anxiety.
- *Carbo vegetabilis* for shock causing clammy hands.
- *Coffea* for insomnia caused by an overactive mind – or too much coffee.
- *Colocynthis* for anger that causes headaches or indigestion.
- *Gelsemium* for shock, or worry that's making you feel irritable and tearful.
- *Ignatia amara* for shock, where you're trying unsuccessfully to stay in control.
- *Kali phosphoricum* for jaded nerves.
- *Stramonium* for a bout of sudden, intense panic.

help. The type of remedy you take will depend on the type of person you are and the worries you have.
- If your mind is working overtime and is crowded with thoughts that won't go away, preventing you from sleeping, or making you wake far too early in the morning, try Nie Vomica 6 or 30.
- If you cannot sleep because your nerves are on edge, try Kali Phos 6x.

- If sleeplessness is being caused by anxiety and fear and you are tossing and turning and waking up between midnight and 2 a.m., try Arsenicum 6 or 30.
- If you cannot sleep because you are worrying about an event that will take place the following day, like a particularly bad meeting at work, or a visit to the dentist for example, try Gelsemium 6 or 30.
- And if you wake up at the slightest sound or are over excited about something, with all your senses on the *qui vive*, try Coffea 6 or 30.

Anxiety

If you are feeling overanxious, homeopathy has remedies which are suited to the type of person you are and the type of anxiety you are suffering:

- If you are in a panic, and full of agitation and restlessness, Aconite 6 or 30 may be the answer for you.
- If you are suffering from diarrhoea caused by anxiety, or you tend to feel claustrophobic or suffer from vertigo, then try Arg Nit 6 or 30.
- If your anxiety is caused by oversensitivity and you are a highly emotional person with dramatic mood swings, try Ignatia 6 or 30.
- If social situations cause you anxiety because you suffer from insecurity and lack of confidence, try Lycopodium 6 or 30.

Irritability

Overwork can make you extremely irritable. Here are some possible homoepathic solutions which will work short term. Again these are suited to your emotional makeup and the nature of the problem.

- For an irritable person who prefers to be left on her own, and feels worse for any kind of movement, try Bryonia 6 or 30.
- For irritability accompanied by a feeling of weakness and backache, try Kali Carb 6 or 30.
- If you are a headstrong, nagging, fault-finding sort of woman and have no patience and are irritated by smells, noise and light, then Nux Vomica 6 or 30 may be the answer for you.
- If you tend to be a bully at home but in the outside world you lack both confidence and decisiveness, and you wake up angry and irritable, try Lycopodium 6 or 30.
- If you are irritable and snap people's heads off just before you have your period, and tend to feel overburdened by demands and easily offended, try Sepia 6 or 30.
- And finally if you are extremely sensitive about what others say about you and feel deep indignation, your problems probably arise because your anger is unexpressed. Try Staphsagria 6 for 20.

Flower Remedies

❦

Even gentler than homeopathy, flower remedies aim to combat stress and illness by balancing our emotional energies. It's easy to see why people should think flowers can heal psychological wounds. Their delicate beauty and fragrance have always been linked with spirituality.

IN THE 1930s, idealistic homeopath Dr Edward Bach (pronounced 'batch') came to believe flowers have an affinity with the human soul and could put people back in tune with their higher natures. This in turn would reduce illness, which is so often caused by mental stresses.

He developed a range of 38 essences, which he believed dealt with every emotional state people could suffer.

The remedies aren't claimed to solve problems directly – how could they? – but are aimed at helping people bring their feelings back into balance.

Since then other practitioners around the world have taken up the idea and there are now about two dozen different ranges containing more than 1,200 remedies. That's everything from New Zealand's abelia, which helps balance our rational and emotional sides, to the African zinnia, which helps us loosen up and re-learn how to laugh. Some cover

From Around the World

Look out for some of the many different ranges now on offer. Several also include emergency remedies.

- Australian Bush Flower Essences include waratah to help deal with stress and use our survival skills, mountain devil for high blood pressure, jacaranda for nervousness and black-eyed Susan for hyper-activity.
- From Findhorn in Scotland come Scottish prim-rose for peace, broom for clarity of mind and thistle for courage.
- Himalayan Indian Tree and Flower Essences include pongham tree to rest the brain, commelina to calm the nerves and red-hot cat tail to prevent over-impulsiveness.
- From Andreas Korte's African and Amazon range; cinnamon rose to restore hope, dandelion for reducing tension and wild carrot to stop thoughts racing around the brain.

aspects Bach didn't deal with, including sexuality.

Bach remedies seem to be the easiest to find – the little bottles are widely sold in pharmacies and health food shops. You can use up to half a dozen at a time, putting a few drops in a drink or straight onto your tongue. Rescue Remedy is the best known – a blend of impatiens, star of Bethlehem, cherry plum, rock rose and clematis to relieve stress and panic in an emergency.

Some remedies contain alcohol as a preservative,

but they're all harmless and can be used alongside any medical treatment.

Bach remedies for stress

The following remedies can have a marked effect on you when you are feeling stressed out. They will help you relax.

At least one of the flower remedies will be suitable for you – however bad your mood.

Impatiens if you're energetic but tense.

Cherry plum if you're on the verge of a breakdown.

Clematis for absent-mindedness caused by withdrawal from the real world.

Rock rose for frozen terror and a sense of helplessness.

Star of Bethlehem for the after-effects of shock.

Agrimony for mental torment behind a brave face.

Aspen for fears of unknown origin.

Elm if overwhelmed by responsibility.

Gorse for despair.

Red chestnut when you're over-concerned for others.

Sweet chestnut for extreme mental anguish.

White chestnut for obsessive worrying.

Wild rose for apathy.

Spas & Beauty Therapy

❈

Beauty treatments can be a real pick-me-up, making you look and feel great. Nothing is more soothing than being pampered. If you automatically think 'I can't do that — it costs too much', are you really broke? Or don't you feel right about 'wasting' money on pleasure for yourself? An occasional treat may not break the budget. Why not phone a few local places and find out?

For some of us it's a hairdo — a gentle head massage and a flattering cut can do as much good as a holiday. And if your hairdresser makes you feel guilty about your split ends, go to someone else next time. Remember you're paying!

Others take refuge in beauty salons, which offer a wider range of comforts such as massage, pedicures, facials and body wraps. Again, it's the mixture of relaxation and beautifying which has such beneficial effects.

Health clubs

Some women don't like hands-on therapies, especially if they've had babies clambering over them all day. For them, a health club is the place. Health clubs offer a variety of facilities for relaxation, including a Jacuzzi, steam room, sauna, as well as massage, reflexology, aromatherapy and beauty therapies. Don't bother with the sunbeds, they can damage your skin – head straight for the warmth and water.

Saunas put out an intense dry heat which some people love. But don't despair if it just brings your skin up in hot blotches – steam rooms are back in fashion now, hiding everyone in clouds of soft vapour. Then shower the sweat off and jump into the swimming pool or Jacuzzi. If you do all this after an aerobics class or game of tennis, of course, you'll have the added glow of virtue.

Float tank

You take a shower, then climb into a bathtub with a lid, or a tiny room like a flooded sauna, and shut yourself in. It's pitch dark and silent.

- You lie on water so salty that you float. Both water and air are at body temperature, so you can't feel anything. With nothing to stimulate your senses you may hallucinate. *And people do this willingly?*
- Actually, it's astonishingly relaxing. You can turn the light on or scramble out whenever you like.
- Not everyone takes to it, but even claustrophobics find themselves letting go of the light cord and drifting peacefully in their own world.
- You may find beautiful or disturbing images well up from your unconscious. You may feel a deep sense of peace and oneness with the world. You may just get bored.
- Some centres play relaxing music and you can also

bring a meditation or self-hypnosis tape – this is one place where you won't be distracted.

Play Safe

If you're pregnant or suffer ill-health, especially a heart or skin condition, please check with your doctor before trying health club treatments. Don't use the float tank if you have mental health problems.

Health resorts

Are you going to a health resort? Congratulations! Shop around for one that meets your needs – some are real old-style fat farms, specializing in quick, short-term weight loss through hunger. Others are geared up for activity, and may help you start a fitness regime that's tailored to your needs.

If relaxation is your main aim, head for somewhere with treatments and facilities you would like to try, preferably in peaceful country surroundings. You could also contact health centres and retreats advertised in New Age magazines, which offer alternative therapies like crystal healing too.

Bath Delights

*Water is our element, just as much as air. It makes up 70
per cent of our bodies, and of the planet. Our long-ago
ancestors evolved in warm seas, as we did in the waters
of the womb. No wonder, that for most of us, sinking into
a warm bath is the most relaxing moment of our day.*

IF YOU LIVE ALONE, put the answering machine on
or unplug the telephone. Otherwise, find a convenient time and let everyone know that you are not to
be interrupted for, say, half an hour. If you have the
place to yourself during the day, why not indulge in a
luxurious afternoon soak? Treat yourself to some big,
thick, fluffy towels and a bathrobe to snuggle into.

Then settle in for the most peaceful experience you
could have. Make sure you will not be disturbed and
float off in your own private world. Make sure the
room is warm, light some candles and turn off the
overhead light. Listen to the sounds of summer in the
garden – or play a tape to create the scene. Put on a
cassette of sea sounds or atmospheric relaxation
music. For fragrance, use a scented candle or some
aromatherapy oil in a burner.

Now's the time to cleanse your skin, smooth on
some moisturizer or a facepack if you like and check

the body lotion is at hand for when you step out. Add your favourite indulgences – foam bath under a running tap, essential oil just as you get in, a splash of your favourite cologne or a herbal treat you've made yourself. Then slip into the water and relax. This is a lovely time to do a foot-to-head relaxation or some affirmations.

Body heat

Water is said to have the most relaxing effects at body temperature – try it and see. If you don't have a thermometer, aim for a temperature at which you can't really tell if your hand's in the water or not when you test it. It may at first seem unpleasantly tepid, but persevere for at least ten minutes, topping up with hot water to keep the temperature constant.

Otherwise, enjoy your bath warm rather than steaming. It's healthier, kinder to the skin, and more relaxing – very hot water has an exhausting effect.

Shower in a forest

- A shower can be a very relaxing experience too, particularly if you put on a cassette of woodland or rainforest sounds.
- Smooth shower gel all over your body, then close your eyes and imagine yourself strolling through a jungle under tropical rainfall.
- Visualize all your tension seeping out onto your skin like dust and being washed away. Lift your face up and enjoy the water flowing all over your skin.

Essential Oils for your Bath

In a warm, steamy room these essential oils release far more scent than in ordinary circumstances, so only very little is required.

According to the Penny Rich book *Practical Aromatherapy*, the ten best all-the-year-round oils for your bath are:

- 5 drops Bergamot (for melancholy and depression)
- 7 drops Camomile (for insomnia or an itchy skin)
- 8 drops Frankincense (calming, mood-sweetening sedative)
- 10 drops Geranium (relaxing but uplifting, energizing)
- 8 drops Jasmine (for apathy, stress and fatigue)
- 10 drops Lavender (relaxing, soothing, positive)
- 8 drops Neroli (anti-depressant)
- 5 drops Patchouli (invigorating and energizing)
- 10 drops Rose (romantic, happiness, pleasure)
- 8 drops Sandalwood (intimate, sensual, mellowing)

- Imagine stepping out of the trees beside a waterfall where the air's full of sparkling drops. Turn the shower on stronger as you visualize entering the waterfall, thinking of scenes like this in films with you as the heroine.
- Can't you just feel the fresh water carrying all your stresses away?

Play safe

- If you don't have a separate loo (with washbasin), it's worth putting that on your list of priorities next time you move house. As well as easing rush-hour pressure on the busiest room, it means no one has to use the bathroom while you're relaxing in it.
- Keep the cassette player a safe distance from any water.

Planning a Relaxation Day

A day at a health spa is something to save up for or put on your birthday wish-list. But with a bit of planning, a group of friends can organize their own relaxation day at little or no cost, using techniques from this book. With pre-recorded tapes, you can even do it by yourself – or invite your best friend.

ONE PERSON NEEDS to be responsible for organizing, but she can still take part in most sections, using tapes where possible. (A psychological tip – people are much less likely to interrupt a tape.) Take the first few minutes of each section to make sure everyone knows what to do, and keep an eye on beginners in case they need help. At the end of the longer sessions, leave five minutes for people to stretch their legs and chat.

Everything should be at a comfortable level for newcomers to relaxation – remind them not to feel stressed if there's anything they can't manage. Oh, and make sure everyone has some idea about the methods you use, so no one fears meditation or yoga is the first step towards a satanic orgy!

If you're asking people to bring lunch to share, sort out who's bringing what so you don't end up with too many packs of identical cheese sandwiches or cakes. Aim for light, healthy food with plenty of fruit and salad, and provide a selection of herbal teas.

Use local resources if possible. Do you know any trained people – a masseuse, reflexologist, yoga or t'ai chi teacher, for example – who'll give an hour of their time in return for lunch and taking part in the rest of the day? A local homeopath, herbalist or other alternative practitioner may also be willing to give a talk and demonstration.

If anyone suffers a health condition, especially epilepsy, high blood pressure or mental health problems, get them to check with their doctor that it's all right to join in.

What you'll need

- A quiet, empty room, big enough for everyone to lie on the floor. It's best with no one else in the house, so people won't feel inhibited or worry about what the kids are up to. Allow time to move furniture if necessary.
- A table or tray, access to hot water and a selection of herbal teas. Do include some decaffeinated coffee and ordinary tea though, for those who'd miss them too much to relax.
- Cushions, and straight-backed chairs for anyone who can't sit on the floor.
- A cassette recorder with peaceful background tapes such as New Age music or the sounds of the sea or woodland, plus dance music and Middle Eastern music for belly dancing.

- Notes or this book as back-up.

Optional:
- Oil if you're doing any massage.
- A tape to sing with.
- Candles and matches.
- Relaxing oils, a burner and spare nightlight candles.
- Pre-recorded cassettes for foot-to-head relaxation and meditation. If you do these 'live', write yourself a script in advance.
- Some spare blankets.
- A timer.

Ask people to bring

- Lunch.
- Rainwear if the weather looks unreliable and some time is to be spent out of doors.
- A blanket to cover them while they're lying down.

On the Day

※

For best results, organize a schedule for your relaxation day in advance and try to stick to it come what may. The timetable here, fitting round school hours, is just an example – you may want to work one out with the people who are going to take part.

ARE YOUR FRIENDS sedentary workers who need more movement? Or exhausted young mothers who'd seize any chance of lying down? Would they like fewer, longer sessions, or a 10–5 day? Aim for variety without too many changes of pace, and remember not to schedule anything physically taxing straight after eating.

The important thing is not to let time dribble away in 'What shall we do next? . . .'

Timetable

Morning
9.30am   Time for a cup of herbal tea while everyone arrives.

9.40am   Focusing. Sit quietly in a circle for five minutes and get in the mood for the day. Then do some head and neck relaxers from pp. 47–48.

Move gently into:
9.50am Breathing exercises, ending with blue colour breathing.

And on to:
10am Seated meditation. Reassure newcomers that it doesn't matter if they don't feel they're meditating properly – just sitting peacefully is useful too.

10.30am Stretch session. Remind everyone to take it gently and never to do jerky movements.

11am Belly dancing – a change of pace with swirly Middle Eastern music – and probably lots of laughter! Wind down with a few minutes of Infinity meditation.

12 noon Lunch.

Afternoon Plan A
12.30pm Go for a walk on a pre-planned route, using the techniques in the Walking section.

1.15pm Back for tea.

1.30pm Voice therapy. Ease into it with humming, then exercises, then chanting or singing along with a tape.

2pm Moving meditation, perhaps finishing with poses from the Yoga section. Or put on some music and dance if everyone's full of energy.

2.40pm Foot-to-head relaxation, lying on the floor under a blanket. Lie peacefully until 2.55, then finish by saying affirmations such as 'I am peaceful, calm and capable'. Have a long leisurely stretch and get up slowly.

2.59pm A huge round of applause for the organizer!

3pm Back to the workaday world, ready for anything.
Or, see Afternoon Plan B

Afternoon Plan B – rain stops play
12.30pm Voice therapy.

1pm Massage. Pair people off to take turns massaging each other's neck and shoulders. If they'd like to try foot massage, demonstrate some simple kneading, squeezing and toe-pulling movements – a foot massage is so relaxing you don't need any brilliant techniques. Just remind everyone to avoid broken skin and to press hard enough not to tickle.

1.45pm Tea break.

2pm Continue as in Plan A.

Relaxation morning or evening

For a three-hour break, use the all-day timetable but leave out the period 12–2.39. In other words – focusing, breathing, meditation, stretch, belly dance and foot-to-head relaxation. If people are tired, replace the belly dance with voice therapy, moving meditation and yoga.

The Most Important Thing

&

*All the techniques in this book are effective ways of
reducing stress and increasing the ability to relax. It's a
question of trying out some that appeal and finding
which ones suit you. You'll probably end up with a
repertoire of options for different situations.*

DON'T FORGET THE MOST important way of
relieving stress – enjoying life. When you're
overworked or weighed down with responsibilities,
having fun slips a long way down the priority list.
That's when you start grabbing at indulgences that
don't even really give pleasure – stuffing food down,
smoking without really noticing you're doing it,
impulse-buying.

Instead, stop and think what you'd really enjoy
doing. It doesn't have to be something you think is
useful or a formal relaxation method.

If you're so out of the habit you can't think what
you'd like, sit down quietly and wait for some options
to float into your mind. A café meal with your best
friend while the kids are at school? Swimming?
Reading a novel in the park? Taking a bus to somewhere you've never been before? Going to bed?
Taking a singing class? Then imagine yourself actually

doing each of these things and spend a while noting how it feels.

Keep with it till you come up with something you can feel yourself enjoying. Then do it!

- Play games. Playing with children is one of the best ways to relax because you can do things their way – run, yell, laugh, fall down and roll on the grass. There's no better way of working off steam. No children around? Play with your partner or a friend. All you need is a football and someone to kick it around with.
- Make a regular date with friends and take it in turns to organize something cheap and easy for fun.
- Take short breaks, like a weekend away or a day in the country. Longer holidays can sometimes be more stressful than relaxing, because of the organization and travelling involved – and because people feel under pressure to enjoy themselves.
- Spend time with your friends, but have things to do when you get some time to yourself to relax.
- Do something you don't usually do:
- Go to the ballet or theatre (tickets are often cheaper early in the week and at matinees).
- Fly a kite or borrow a pair of skates.
- Take someone's dog for a run.
- Get your friends together and go to a comedy club.
- Go bird-watching.
- Get your partner to join you on a long country walk ending in the pub.

Bringing back the balance

- If you're rushed and disorganized, the slowing relaxation techniques will help you make space in your life. Meditation and breathing exercises, in their various forms, are ideal.

- If you tend to be very controlled, or get depressed and brood about problems, try some of the livelier techniques such as belly dancing or aerobics. Tune your radio to a pop station and do the wildest dance you've ever seen. Sing at the top of your voice (all right, start off quietly and work up). Run on the spot for a minute, then turn the movement into a silly dance.

Shopping to Relax

You don't need any equipment at all to relax. But if you feel like treating yourself or starting a birthday list, the items on these pages were created to aid relaxation.

HEALTH FOOD SHOPS are a good place to start – they stock books, essential oils and all kinds of relaxation aids as well as food. With more people taking an interest in alternative healing, pharmacies too may sell homeopathic medicines, flower remedies and essential oils. Department stores have many of the electrical items. And health and beauty shops stock all kinds of massage-related goods.

To burn oil you can buy candle-fuelled pottery burners from craft stalls and health food shops, or larger electric versions from department stores. Another handy little electric gadget is a negative ionizer, which many people find refreshes the air.

To help with massage, there's a vast range of sophisticated electric devices that knead your muscles tirelessly. Nowadays there's so much choice – vibrating hairbrushes, cushions, chairs, beds, you name it – that it's worth trying out different models. At the simple end of the scale are small, low-cost wooden rollers that do a similar job with muscle power.

Even if you don't suffer from back ache, specialist back-care shops and catalogues have a lot of comfortable furniture and other items – apart from aiding relaxation now, they could prevent back problems starting. Chinese and novelty shops may stock pairs of metal balls with tiny bells inside, to roll in one hand with tranquillizing effects. Wind chimes and indoor fountains can create a peaceful ambience too.

Feet get such a bad deal in everyday life that they come in for a lot of special treatment in the relaxation world. Look out for massage sandals, spiky rollers, vibrating electric pads, miniature whirlpools and all kinds of potions to rub into them. No more than they deserve.

But the kindest thing you can do for your feet, or your back, is to sink into a Banana Chair. This extraordinary-looking device is one of the most comfortable pieces of furniture ever made – you simply lie in it with your feet up, perfectly supported, then put on some peaceful music and drift away. It is wonderfully relaxing.

Relaxation tapes are now so widely available that you can take your pick of styles, accents, with or without music, from a variety of shops or by mail order. There are all kinds of variations on the muscle-relaxation theme, with accompanying visualizations.

The same is true for hypnotherapy tapes, covering stress-relief as well as giving up smoking, gaining confidence and just about anything else you could want to do. One popular series is by British hypnotherapist Jean Credland, whose reassuring, down-to-earth voice makes the whole process feel wonderfully natural. Her *Rainbow Meditation* tape uses colour imagery, as does American Nancy Hopps's *Relaxation/Affirmation Techniques*.

The same shops and catalogues tend to sell relaxing music tapes and CDs, including ambient, ethnic and sounds from nature. Lose yourself in some tribal drumming for moving meditation, or join in with chanting Tibetan monks.

Where Do I Go from Here?

❈

*The safest way to find a local practitioner is through
personal recommendation or by sending an SAE
to a reputable organization, including those
mentioned on these pages.*

IT IS ESPECIALLY IMPORTANT to take care with
hypnotherapy or hands-on treatments, which
could be harmful if done incorrectly. Ask the practitioner in advance about his or her qualifications, costs
and what the treatment involves.

Unlike doctors or nurses, alternative practitioners
don't legally have to know anything about their
subject. Anyone can set up a training school or award
meaningless qualifications, so letters after people's
names may not always be a sign of expertise.

People often visit alternative practitioners when
they're going through a bad patch. In situations like
that it's easy for an unscrupulous person to take
advantage, or convince people they should do whatever the 'expert' says. It's rare, but it has happened,
so if you feel uncomfortable just leave.

For more information about various therapies

Send a stamped, self-addressed envelope to:

The Institute for Complementary Medicine
PO Box 194, London SE16 1QZ, UK, tel 0171-237 5165
(SAE and two loose stamps). Practitioners of various
alternative therapies can take an ICM exam, marked
by independent assessors. If successful, they can join
the British Register of Complementary Practitioners
and put the letters BRCP after their name in addition
to their existing qualification.

The Australian Traditional Medicine Society
PO Box 422, Ryde, New South Wales 2112, Australia.

American Holistic Medical Association
4101 Lake Boone Trail, Ste 201, Raleigh, NC 27607, US,
tel: (919) 787 5181.

Holistic Health Directory
Published by New Age Journal (address page 180)
lists US practitioners state by state.

Standing up to STRESS

Smokers' Quitline
tel: 0171-487 3000.

The National Council for Voluntary Organisations
Regents Wharf, 8 All Saints Street, London N1 9AL.

Essential Health for Women by Sharon Walker
(Robinson).

PMS

Women's Nutritional Advisory Service
PO Box 268, Lewes, East Sussex BN7 2QN, UK, tel: 01273 487366.
Beat PMS Through Diet by Maryon Stewart (Vermilion).

Peaceful pregnancy

Healthy Parents, Healthy Baby by Maryon Stewart (Headline).
Alexander Technique Birth Book by Machover & Drake (Robinson).

Relax? With kids like mine?

Hyperactive Children's Support Group
71 Whyke Lane, Chichester, West Sussex PO19 2LD, UK, tel: 01903 725182.

Mothers and Others for a Livable Planet
40 W20th Street, New York, NY 10011, US, tel: (212) 242 0010.

Moving with the Change

Breezing through the Change by Ellen Brown and Lynne Walker (Frog Ltd).
The Pause by Lonnie Barbach (Bantam).

Coping with Pain

Pain Relief Foundation
Rice Lane, Walton, Liverpool L9 1AE, UK, tel: 0151-523 1486. Information including mail order relaxation and pain-relief audio tapes. Send large SAE.

Organize to avoid stress

How to Make Life Easy for Yourself by Denise Katz (Angus and Robertson).

LETSLINK UK
Liz Shepherd, c/o 61 Woodstock Road, Warminster, Wiltshire BA12 9DH, UK. Information about alternative currencies; organized schemes to barter goods and services.

Taking it from the top

Eva Fraser's Facial Workout (Penguin).

Massage

The Book of Massage by Lucinda Lidell (Ebury).
The Massage Manual by Fiona Harrold (Headline).

American Massage Therapy Association
820 Davis Street, Suite 100, Evanston, IL 60201, US, tel: (708) 864 0123.

Associated Bodywork and Massage Professionals
28677 Buffalo Park Road, Evergreen, CO 80439-7347, US, tel: (303) 674-8478.

Self-massage

Self-Massage by Monika Struna and Connie Church (Vermilion).
Self-Massage by Jacqueline Young (Thorsons).

Shiatsu

The Art of Shiatsu by Oliver Cowmeadow (Element).
Do-It-Yourself Shiatsu by Wataru Ohashi (Unwin).

Aromatherapy

International Federation of Aromatherapists
Stamford House, 2–4 Chiswick High Road, London W4 1TH, UK. Send £2 and A5 SAE.

International Federation of Aromatherapists
25 Singleton Road, North Baldwyn, Victoria 3104, Australia.

National Association for Holistic Aromatherapy
PO Box 17622, Boulder, CO 80308-6799, US.

The Aromatherapy Organisations Council
3 Latymer Close, Braybrooke, Market Harborough, Leics LE16 8LN, UK, tel: 01858 434242.
Practical Aromatherapy by Penny Rich (Robinson).
Aromatherapy: an A–Z by Patricia Davis (CW Daniel UK).
Aromatherapy by Julie Sadler (Ward Lock).
Aromatherapy and the Mind by Julia Lawless (Thorsons).

Reflexology

Association of Reflexologists
27 Old Gloucester Street, London WC1, UK, tel: 0181-451 2218.

International Institute of Reflexology
PO Box 12642, St Petersburg, FL 33733, US, tel: (813) 343 4811.
Reflexology: Foot Massage for Total Health by Inge Dougans with Suzanne Ellis (Element).
Step by Step Reflexology by Renée Tanner (Douglas Barry Publications, 21 Laud Street, Croydon, Surrey CR0 1SU, UK).

Alexander technique

North American Society of Teachers of the Alexander Technique
PO Box 517, Urbana, IL 61801, US, tel: (800) 473 0620.
Alexander Technique by Chris Stevens (Optima).
Body Know-How by Jonathan Drake (Thorsons).

Yoga

Yoga Therapy by Stella Weller (Thorsons).
Yoga for Common Ailments by Drs R Nagarathna, HR Nagendra and Robin Monro (Gaia).

T'ai chi

Tai Chi by Danny Connor (Stanley Paul).

Infinite Tai Chi video by Jason Chan from Talking Pictures, PO Box 77, Cirencester, Glos GL7 5YN, UK.

Exercise

Exercise Association
Unit 4 Angel Gate, City Road, London EC1V 2PT, UK, tel: 0171-278 0811. Qualified instructors.

Sports Council
16 Upper Woburn Place, London WC1H 0QP, UK, tel: 0171-273 1500.

American Council on Exercise
5820 Oberlin Drive, Suite 102, San Diego, CA 92121-3787, US, tel: (619) 535 8227.

Fitness Industry Association
PO Box 60, Arncliffe, New South Wales 2205, Australia, tel: (02) 9212 7185.
Keep Moving! It's Aerobic Dance by Esther Kan and Minda Goodman Kraines (Mayfield).
Health & Fitness magazine, Nexus House, Azalea Drive, Swanley, Kent BR8 8HY, UK, tel: 01322 660070.

Stretch

The Complete Book of Stretching by Tony Lycholat (Crowood UK).

Belly dance

Sorra Enterprises
The White Cottage, High Street, Harwell Village, Oxon OX11 0EX, UK, tel: 01235 834073. Music tapes, costumes, books and information on classes.
Belly Dancing for Health and Relaxation by Tina Hobin (Duckworth UK).

Autogenic training

The British Association for Autogenic Training and Therapy
18 Holtsmere Close, Watford, Herts WD2 6NG, UK.
Autogenic Training by Dr Kai Kermani (Thorsons).

Meditation

Meditation for Everybody by Louis Proto (Penguin).
Meditation, a Treasury of Technique by Pam and Gordon Smith (CW Daniel).
The Everyday Meditator by Osho (Boxtree).

Mindfulness

Ad Brugman
The Orchard, Lower Maescoed, Hereford HR2 0HP, UK, tel: 01873 860207. Runs mindfulness courses.
The Experience of Insight by Joseph Goldstein (Unity Press).
The Miracle of Mindfulness by Thich Nhat Hanh (Beacon).

Moving meditation

The Everyday Meditator by Osho (Boxtree).
The Serpent and the Wave by Jalaja Bonheim (Celestial Arts).

Raven Recordings
744 Broad Street, Room 1815, Newark, New Jersey 07102, US, tel: (201) 642 7942 and Raven Recordings, Staccato, Bridam, Kents Road, Wellswood, Torquay TQ1 2NN, UK, tel: 01803 295442. Music tapes and videos by Gabrielle Roth, guru of modern meditation.

Five to Midnight
Nappers Crossing, Staverton, South Devon TQ9 6PD, UK. Moving meditation.

Self-hypnosis

Self-Hynosis Step by Step by J. P. Guyonnand (Souvenir Press).
Self-Hynosis by Valerie Austin (Thorsons).

Colour therapy

Susan Farrar
The Iris Centre, 10 Princes Road, London SW14 8PE, UK, tel: 0181 876 2548.
The Book of Colour Healing by Theo Gimbel (Gaia Books).

Voice therapy

Susan Lever
2 Woodlea, Coulby Newham, Middlesbrough TS8 0TX, UK, tel: 01642 590562. Workshops, sound healing and voice therapy tapes.

Frankie Armstrong
45 Cecil Street, Cardiff CF2 1NW, UK, tel: 01222 480429. Singing and voice workshops.

Mim Beim
Sydney, Australia, tel (02) 211 3811. Naturopathy and voice work.

Voice Movement Therapy Association
PO Box 4218, London SE22 0JE, UK.
The Book of Sound Therapy by Olivea Dewhurst-Maddock (Gaia).

Herbalism

The National Institute of Medical Herbalists
56 Longbrook Street, Exeter, Devon EX4 6AH, UK.

The General Council and Register of Consultant Herbalists
Marlborough House, Swanpool, Falmouth, Cornwall TR11 4HW, UK.

Baldwin & Co
171 Walworth Road, London SE17 1RW, UK. Herbal supplier.

Herbal Remedies by Christopher Hedley & Non Shaw (Robinson).

The Herb Society's Home Herbal by Penelope Ody (Dorling Kindersley).

Herbal Healing for Women by Rosemary Gladstar (Bantam).

The Herbal for Mother and Child by Anne McIntyre (Element).

Homeopathy

The British Homeopathic Association
27a Devonshire Street, London W1N 1RJ, UK, tel: 0171 935 2163. Medically qualified homeopaths.

The Society of Homeopaths
2 Artizan Road, Northampton NN1 4HU, UK, tel: 01604 21400. Lay homeopaths.

The Family Encyclopedia of Homeopathic Remedies by Peter Webb (Robinson).

Practical Homeopathy by Sylvia Tracher (Robinson).

The Complete Guide to Homeopathy by Dr Andrew Lockie and Dr Nicola Geddes (Dorling Kindersley).

Homoeopathy: Heart and Soul by Dr Keith Souter (CW Daniel).

Homoeopathic First Aid by Dr Anne Clover (Thorsons).

Flower remedies

International Federation for Vibrational Medicine
Middle Piccadilly Natural Healing Centre, Holwell, nr Sherborne, Dorset DT9 5LW, UK, tel: 01963 23468.

The Dr E Bach Centre
Mount Vernon, Sotwell, Wallingford, Oxon OX10 0PZ, UK, tel: 01491 834678.

International Flower Essence Repertoire
The Working Tree, Milland, Liphook, Hants, GU30 7JS, UK, tel: 01428 741672. Remedies by mail order.

Nelson Bach USA
Dept NJ95, 1007 West Upsal Street, Philadelphia, PA 19119, US, tel: 1-800-314 BACH.

The Australian Flower Remedy Society
PO Box 531, Spit Junction, New South Wales 2088, Australia.
The Encyclopaedia of Flower Remedies by Clare G Harvey and Amanda Cochrane (Thorsons).

Spa and beauty therapy

Healthy Venues
UK, tel: 01203 690300. Bookings for many health resorts, including treatments.

Spa Finders
US, fax: (212) 924 7240. Bookings for health resorts.

Shopping

Jean Credland

Rainbows, 7 Baile Hill Terrace, York YO1 1HF, tel: 01904 629024.

Nancy Hopps
Synergistic Systems, PO Box 5224, Eugene, OR 97405, US.

New World Cassettes
Paradise Farm, Westhall, Halesworth, Suffolk IP19 8RH, UK. Mail order.

New World Productions
PO Box 244 WBO, Red Hill, Queensland 4059, Australia, tel: (07) 3367 0788. Mail order music.

Mysteries
9 Monmouth Street, London WC2H 9DA, UK, tel: 0171-240 3688. Shop and mail order, many relaxation items.

Educating Hands Bookstore
261 SW 8th Street, Miami, Florida 33130, US, tel: (305) 285 0651. Shop and mail order books, tapes, videos and more.

Quintessential Oils
847 35th Street, Richmond CA 94805, US. Massage and herbal products.

And more . . .

All kinds of treatments, goods, holidays, workshops and mail order catalogues are advertised in magazines such as:

Kindred Spirit
Foxhole, Dartington, Totnes, Devon TQ9 6EB, UK,
tel: 01803 866686.

New Age Journal
42 Pleasant Street, Watertown, MA 02172, US, tel:
(617) 926 0200.

Australian WellBeing Holistic Centre
Freepost 3, PO Box 249, Mosman, NSW 2088,
Australia, tel: (02) 9922 7811.